GROW
IN FAITH
TOWARD
MATURITY

GROW IN FAITH TOWARD MATURITY

31 DAYS TO A CLOSER WALK WITH GOD

DEBORAH J. NAYROCKER

Deborah J. Nayrocker

credo
house publishers

Grow in Faith toward Maturity

Copyright © 2017 by Deborah J. Nayrocker

All rights reserved

Published in the United States by Credo House Publishers,
a division of Credo Communications, LLC, Grand Rapids, Michigan
www.credohousepublishers.com

ISBN: 978-1-625860-86-6

Cover and interior design by Sharon VanLoozenoord
Editing by Elizabeth Banks

Printed in the United States of America

First edition

Contents

Preface

How often do you examine your relationship with God? God invites us to enjoy a deeper relationship with him. We can experience our heavenly Father's love and presence every day. The disciple James said, if we draw close to God, he will draw close to us.

Grow in Faith toward Maturity consists of thirty-one chapters, or brief readings, designed for daily devotional use. As you read these chapters, my hope is that you will not only understand more about God, but you also will love God more. And when you love him more you will want to please him by living a holy and disciplined life. He empowers you to be what he created you to be.

This book includes true stories from my life. I've written the events as I've recalled them. I've changed some people's names but not their stories. I spent many of my childhood and teenage years living in Brazil. My father was a minister in the United States and Brazil. My mother had an active ministry role working with him. I share some of our experiences of how I've witnessed God working mightily.

I'm hopeful this book will inspire you to be intentional as you grow in your relationship with God. I pray you come to be convinced that God can continue to make a difference in your life.

PART ONE
Accept Him

CHAPTER 1

Begin with the Living Water

"With joy you will draw water from the wells of salvation."

ISAIAH 12:3

What if I told you there is nothing more important in life than making one very important decision? And, furthermore, that this decision is a life-and-death decision, an eternal decision.

Believers understand this basic teaching—if we repent of our sins and believe in Jesus Christ as our Savior we'll go to heaven. Yes, this is a wonderful promise and mystery. But can you imagine not moving on from this foundational teaching? Can you imagine not moving on to become mature believers and to enjoy all that God is calling each of us to be?

Regrettably, there are many believers today who are content to stay as they were when they became newborn Christians. Even now they remain undernourished and spiritually weak. Their growth has been curtailed and stunted. And most tragic of all, they show no longing to know God better.

Some Christians struggle in their walk, failing to enjoy a real and consistent relationship with God. Too often they consider the act of salvation to be an intellectual decision and not a transformational one. Looking at their lives, one sees little spiritual growth. Some of them don't sense a connection or closeness to God, even doubting he works in the world today.

Too many believers are trying to live as Christians without maturing in their relationship with God. At one time they were quite aware of God's gentle nudgings. Now it seems they are no longer curious to know what Scriptures say about flourishing in the Christian life.

How can this be, when it is our goal as believers to be well pleasing to God? Do we have an eternal perspective, desiring to live to please our Lord and Savior? Or could our relationship with God be superficial?

We know it is the same great power of God that brings about our newfound faith *and* enables us to continue to change and grow.

The Bible says, "And without faith it is impossible to please God, because anyone who comes to him must believe that he exists and that he rewards those who earnestly seek him."[1] God rewards us when we earnestly seek him. When we casually seek him we are not going to grow and change.

Christians are called to spiritual maturity in Christ. Our spiritual formation comes from a close relationship with God. He desires that our faith in him should grow so we can experience his promises and blessings.

In this book we will look closely at how to be strong in our Christian faith. We will:

❖ focus on specific actions to take to grow as believers;
❖ become aware of how God is working in us and how he changes us to be more Christlike;
❖ grow to have a closer relationship with our heavenly Father;
❖ learn to experience God's daily presence in our lives; and
❖ walk toward the goal of holiness.

Throughout this book we will explore God's Word, examining biblical principles and stories that move us to have a deeper life with God. The book is divided into eight parts. Each part focuses on an important way to be intentional in our spiritual formation, developing Christlike character. They are: (1) Accept him. (2) Trust in him. (3) Be transformed by him. (4) Abide in him. (5) Love him. (6) Walk with him. (7) Live for him. (8) Rest in him.

Someone who is searching for something more in life is like a person who can't wait to have his or her thirst quenched. I recall my experience of thirsting for amazing cold water.

Did you ever drink water that was so cool and refreshing you wanted more of it? Was it freshly drawn from an outside well? I've experienced this.

As a young girl I liked visiting my friend Laura. She lived on a farm near our small town. It was the old-fashioned lifestyle of the farm I liked most. Everyone pitched in to do his part.

Laura's father planted crops in the field across the road from their house. I watched him plow the land, guiding the plow pulled by a horse. Laura's mother often stitched new clothes for the family with her sewing machine, powered by a foot pedal. The children helped raise goats, pigs, and chickens.

There was no running water in their simple home. Instead, the family drew water from a well for everyday needs.

Especially on hot days, I looked forward to drinking a cup of cool water from my friend's well. Laura would drop the empty pail into the deep well, with a long rope attached to it. After what seemed like minutes, the pail would hit the water's surface at the bottom. Once the pail was full, Laura slowly lifted the heavy pail to the very top. Then she carefully poured fresh, glistening water into my cup, quenching my thirst for a while.

Like my friend who lived on a farm, people have gone to wells to fetch water for generations.

I am reminded of the story of Jesus who stopped one day at Jacob's well. The beloved disciple John wrote an eyewitness account of this story in John chapter four.

Let's meet someone who was searching for something more in her life. Although the answer to a fulfilling life had been passed down in her family for generations, she did not yet understand it.

Then one day she met a kind stranger. She listened raptly to him and received a message of hope. It changed her life forever.

The Request at Jacob's Well

One day Jesus left Judea and headed north to Galilee. He took the direct route, passing through the land of Samaria. Since the people of Samaria were a mixed race, part Jew and Gentile, the Orthodox Jews usually avoided that area. At one time the people of Samaria knew the truths about God and worshiped him. Then they allowed people who worshiped other gods to settle among them.

Many of Jesus' teachings came through his friendly and warm encounters with people. One such encounter started with a conversation and a simple request for water.

One day at six o'clock in the evening, Jesus stopped at Jacob's well in the town of Sychar. Tired from his travels, he sat alone at the well. His disciples left to buy food in town.

Then a woman came to draw water at her usual time. To her surprise, Jesus asked her for a drink. It was an unusual request. "You are a Jew and I am a Samaritan woman. How can you ask me for a drink?"[2] she responded.

Jesus used a commonplace word, *water*, to teach a profound meaning. His request led to a conversation that dealt specifically with her. She could relate to the necessity of water, since she spent hours each day carrying jugs of water to and from the well.

Jesus answered, "If you knew the gift of God and who it is that asks you for a drink, you would have asked him and he would have given you living water."[3]

We learn about the woman from Sychar from her interview with Jesus.

She Has a Rich Family Heritage

How could Jesus get water that was more satisfying than the water she drew from Jacob's well? she wondered. After all, her ancestral father Jacob drank from that same well. For generations, their flocks and herds had drunk from it.

She had been told many adventurous stories of Jacob's life. He had been deceitful and manipulative in his younger years. But then, after an encounter with an angel, Jacob emerged a different man. He became a more likable and more honorable person. His name was changed to Israel.

She Is Observant

When the woman from Sychar first saw Jesus, she noticed right away he was a rabbi from another area. Then Jesus said he offered something better than material water. He gave living water, quenching the thirst of everyone who drank of it. The water he gives, Jesus explained, "will become in him a spring of water welling up to eternal life."[4] She knew then, from the way he spoke, that this man was even greater than her ancestor Jacob.

She Is Searching for Something More

Then the woman from Samaria asked Jesus for this living water. After all, it was laborious for her to go to the well every day. He told her to get her husband and return. She answered she had no husband.

Then Jesus said, "You are right when you say you have no husband."[5] He told her he knew she had had five previous husbands, and she was just living with a man at the time. Taken aback at what he knew about her, she realized then he was also a prophet.

Yes, she was looking for love and hadn't found it in her previous relationships. She was looking for someone to take away the emptiness in her life. In her heart she still felt empty. She admitted what Jesus said was true.

She Has a Religious Background

The Samaritan woman soon turned the discussion to focus on their religious differences. She asked Jesus about the right place of worship.

Jesus told her that neither the Samaritans' shrine on Mount Gerizim nor the Jerusalem Temple was the only right place to worship. Speaking with authority, he said salvation was from the Jews. He added, "True worshipers will worship the Father in spirit and truth, for they are the kind of worshipers the Father seeks."[6] Worship comes from a sincere and genuine heart.

Throughout her life the Samaritan woman had known all about religious matters. But it didn't change the way she lived her life. She had continued to sin.

She Is Hopeful

Then the woman excitedly told Jesus something she knew for sure. Having heard of a coming Savior, she told Jesus, "I know that

Messiah" (called Christ) "is coming. When he comes, he will explain everything to us."[7] Then Jesus said, "I who speak to you am he."[8]

His words spoke to her heart. By this time, she knew he was more than a prophet. From the beginning of her conversation with Jesus, her knowledge of him continued to grow. Finally, her eyes were opened and she became aware she was speaking to Christ the Messiah.

She Accepts the Messiah

Jesus' words convicted her and she repented. She didn't need to hope anymore for the coming Messiah. She had seen him!

The woman from Sychar could not contain her joy. Leaving her water jars behind at the well, she went back immediately to town, telling the people about her encounter with the Messiah. He had quenched her soul's thirst. Jesus had brought a dramatic change to her life.

Jesus revealed his truths to the woman, the first non-Jew to become a believer. Because of her zeal and testimony, many of the Samaritans went to the outskirts of town to the well. They wanted to hear and see for themselves this man who made a difference in their friend's life. Many of the villagers believed in Jesus Christ.

They heard the message that Jesus brings new life to a lost world. He offers good news to all. Jesus said, "I am the resurrection and the life. He who believes in me will live, even though he dies; and whoever lives and believes in me will never die. Do you believe this?"[9]

How did Jesus interact with this woman from Sychar? He spoke to her as a friend. The love of Jesus breaks down barriers. Patiently, Jesus talked with the woman. With compassion and love, he engaged in a discussion with her on the fine points of theology. Jesus reached across the cultural barriers of his day to speak respectfully to her. He didn't chastise her, but he was forgiving, Instead of condemning her, he offered her a new way of life.

In the same way, he reaches across the barrier of our sins with its wages of death, and offers eternal life. Desiring to exclude no one, Jesus offers salvation to all. It does not matter what one's status or race is in society. Scripture says, "The Lord is . . . patient with you, not wanting anyone to perish, but everyone to come to repentance."[10]

The Father God's heart and desire is that no one should live without him and the abundant life he offers. The Lord God wants salvation and redemption for everyone. He wants everyone to know him, enjoying a close relationship with him. His presence is real to the ones who seek him and accept him completely.

The Samaritan woman had hollow substitutes for that which wholly satisfies. But then she found her identity and strength at the Source of the living water. After meeting her Savior, she tapped into a new way of life. She accepted the friendship Jesus offered her.

Forsaking God, many people today are drinking from wells that do not satisfy. Pursuing things they thought would satisfy, they have bitter substitutes. They have not gone to the Source of refreshing, living water.

What are some distasteful substitutes you have pursued?

Perhaps you may have settled for hearing the stories of how God worked in the lives of people in generations past. You may know where your fathers worshiped God, as the Samaritan woman did. Although she had some religious beliefs, she appeared to live in a manner contrary to them.

Families may have a Christian heritage. Yet perhaps they live in a dry and empty land, not wholly satisfied. Appearing to live moral lives, some folks may depend on mere outward formalities. They may be missing authentic righteousness in their inner person. Such lives are as empty as the water jars hauled day after day to Jacob's well.

True believers have had an inward spiritual experience in the heart that enlivens and satisfies, bringing meaning and purpose.

What is evident from this story of Jesus and the woman of Samaria? The more time spent with Jesus, the more that can be learned about him. He will reveal more about the matters of the heart. Believers will gain more understanding of his ways.

Water, a symbol of life and abundance, brings refreshment and satisfaction. A thirst for satisfaction in life is quenched only by the living water. Jesus said, "Blessed are those who hunger and thirst for righteousness, for they will be filled."[11] Are you receiving refreshment from the living water? Has Jesus brought satisfaction in your life, filling the emptiness?

The springs of living water bring real hope and joy. Joy is a fruit of the Spirit, and it defies circumstances. When you drink deeply from the fountain of salvation, you are spiritually satiated.

Prayer
Dear God, thank you for being patient with me. Help me not to forsake you. Help me hunger and thirst for righteousness. Thank you for providing abundant life to me. Amen.

Scripture for Further Meditation
Psalm 16:11; John 6:35; John 7:37

Takeaway
When you accept God into your life, he brings salvation and satisfaction through his Son Jesus Christ.

CHAPTER 2

Acknowledge That Jesus Paid It All

"He himself bore our sins in his body on the tree,
so that we might die to sins and live for righteousness."

1 PETER 2:24

Many years ago you and I were taken hostage in the garden of Eden. We became hostages when Adam and Eve were not satisfied in God or in what he offered them. They were cleverly tempted and enticed into sin. Deceived, they thought life would be better and fuller their way. As they stood by the tree, they ate of the forbidden fruit. Because of their disobedience the first man and woman were banished from the beautiful garden. They didn't enjoy paradise anymore. They were alienated from God.

Consequently, we were born sinners, separated from God. We've been held captive and we haven't been able to free ourselves on our own.

Through that abduction, the evil hostage taker took every one of Adam and Eve's descendants into captivity. That includes you and me.

We know that no one is born righteous. Tragically, we were born with a rebellious and sinful nature. Affected by Adam's sin, we have all missed the mark. The prophet Isaiah said, "Your iniquities have separated you from your God."[1] The apostle Paul repeated this truth when he said, "All have sinned and fall short of the glory of God."[2]

In the Old Testament, animal sacrifices were required as appeasement to God. These offerings were made to cover one's iniquities. Paul stated, "What the law was powerless to do in that it was weakened by the sinful nature, God did by sending his own Son in the likeness of sinful man to be a sin offering."[3]

Since we are dead in our trespasses and sins, we need a cure. We are stuck in the mire of our sinful nature. But unless we know we are dead in our sins, we won't look for a cure.

Fortunately, there is an answer. Reaching out to all, God has made a complete cure available to mankind. Through his grace, God has removed spiritual death, bringing righteousness.

More than 2,000 years ago Jesus Christ bore the marks of suffering for us. He was arrested and mocked. He was beaten mercilessly. Then Jesus was forced to carry his cross for execution. Along the way, the Roman soldiers demanded a bystander named Simon carry the cross for Jesus. Apparently Jesus was too weak to carry it himself.

Then Jesus Christ was nailed to the cross at Calvary. His final words were, "It is finished."[4] He died in our place as an atonement for our sins, taking upon himself our guilt.

God sent Jesus to appease his wrath for all of humanity. Yes, Jesus satisfied the wrath of God. Why did he do this? Christ freely took the wrath upon himself so we could have access to God.

Jesus is the Lamb whom God provided. We can rejoice that Jesus was willing to take upon himself our sins on the cross at Calvary. The precious blood of Jesus was shed for us and cleanses us. Christ died in the place of the unjust to bring us to the holy and just God. Suffering in our place, he paid the penalty for our unrighteousness.

We were once held captive by the enemy's wiles. But God's payment to redeem us was made complete. Christ was man; he was the second Adam. He paid our ransom and set us free.

We are no longer under the penalty of the law thanks to Christ's death and resurrection. John the Baptist stated, "For the law was given through Moses; grace and truth came through Jesus Christ."[5]

Grace came through Jesus Christ. He loved us enough to die for us. Isaiah said, "We all, like sheep, have gone astray, each of us has turned to his own way, and the LORD has laid on him the iniquity of us all."[6]

Truth also came through Jesus Christ. God "wants all men to be saved and to come to a knowledge of the truth. For there is one God and one mediator between God and men, the man Christ Jesus, who gave himself as a ransom for all men—the testimony given in its proper time."[7] This ransom payment was complete and successful.

The two Greek verbs for *redeem* mean "to release on receipt of a ransom" or "to buy out." When we become children of God, we are set free from the power of sin. The bondage was broken by the one intermediary, Jesus Christ. No longer hopeless in this world, we have received a divine gift.

Pastor and author George Duncan spoke on the price of salvation. He said, "The price was what one of our great theologians has called 'the infinite worth of the Son of God.' There was a price because there was a penalty to be borne. But there is a further cost to be borne because salvation is more than forgiveness—we are not only guilty, we are sinful. We need more than forgiveness. What good is forgiveness to me if I am going to go on sinning? I need more than pardon. I need power. . . . A life was laid down so that the penalty would be met. A life is lived out in our hearts so that a remedy may be found. This is no cheap tawdry salvation that God gives. It is a wonderful gift, a costly gift, a royal gift, a divine gift."[8]

Not only has Christ forgiven our sins, but he also has removed the reign of sin in our lives. He has replaced it with the internal power of God's Holy Spirit. Paul said, "Count yourselves dead to sin but alive to God in Christ Jesus. Therefore do not let sin reign in your mortal body so that you obey its evil desires. . . . For sin shall not be your master, because you are not under law, but under grace."[9]

Maybe you remember a day years ago when you were saved. You knew God had come into your life. But today you are still letting sin reign. It smothers you.

God is now your Master and you are no longer a slave to sin. You are free to live with no condemnation or forthcoming penalties. Being made righteous, you are dead to guilt and shame. God has been true to his promise: "I will forgive their wickedness and snow.

We all must recognize who we are. We are sinners who need God's grace. When we confess our sins to God we are cleansed. Justified freely by his grace, we have been redeemed through Jesus Christ.

There is no need to work for our salvation. We accept God's gift of salvation, the finished work on the cross. We rejoice in the once-for-all sacrifice of Christ.

Spiritually, are you living in a lovely home or in slum-like conditions? Jesus has set you free. Is there any area of your life you feel is still keeping you captive?

God's Holy Spirit has come to indwell within you. You are now set free to live a holy life, acceptable to God.

Prayer

Gracious Lord, I am thankful Christ gave himself to ransom me from the slavery of sin. He took upon himself my guilt and iniquities. I'm thankful you have released me from the enemy's power, paying the penalty for my sins. Amen.

Scripture for Further Meditation

Isaiah 53:6; Matthew 1:21; John 8:36; Romans 3:21–26; Hebrews 10:1–10

Takeaway

When you accept God's wonderful gift of salvation, you are forever set free from the power of sin.

CHAPTER 3

Believe in Jesus Christ

"Believe in the Lord Jesus, and you will be saved—you and your household."

ACTS 16:31

I've known people who thought being religious was good enough for them to move on in life. But when they were faced with difficult times and pressed with questions about God and life, their doubts set in. They knew they were missing something. Often their search led them to different relationships, careers, or places. It led them away from God. And then it often led them to the one true God.

God accepts us—just as we are. Are we willing to accept him—totally and wholeheartedly?

There's a story of a missionary working on a translation of the book of John. Working in an African dialect, he had difficulty finding the right word for the expression *believe*. He left it blank.

One day a young lad arrived at his village, tired from running for hours from another village. He came with an important message and quickly blurted it out upon his arrival. Exhausted from his long trek, he flung himself in a nearby hammock, saying a word that was new to the translator.

The missionary asked the villagers for the word's meaning. "It means *I am resting all my weight here*," one of them replied.

"Thank God! That is exactly the word I need for *believe*," said the missionary. He had been searching for a word to describe how we depend fully and completely on Jesus Christ for his grace and forgiveness. Now he could complete the translation.

Paul and Silas were two early Christians who boldly used the word *believe* when they spread the good news. Unafraid, they visited several cities along the Mediterranean Sea.

One day Paul and Silas were in the city of Philippi in Macedonia when they were falsely accused of crimes. Certain people in the Roman city were hostile to Paul and Silas. They dragged them into the marketplace to the authorities. The city magistrates tore the robes off Paul and Silas and gave orders to beat the men with rods. After a heavy beating Paul and Silas were thrown into prison. There, they were confined to an inner cell with their feet in stocks.

Even though Paul and Silas had just been severely beaten and thrown in prison, they prayed and sang. At midnight, an earthquake opened the prison doors. Yet, no prisoners escaped.

The jailer, having feared for his life, was relieved. But the close call that night led the jailer to go to Paul and Silas for answers. The jailer of Philippi knew of their preaching. For that is why they were mercilessly beaten and thrown into prison. Yet, the jailer heard these persecuted men singing hymns and praying to God throughout the night. No doubt the jailer observed the peace these men displayed during their confinement.

Having seen Paul and Silas's example of great faith, the jailer asked them, "Sirs, what must I do to be saved?"[1] The men didn't say, "Well, first you need to follow this list of obligatory rules." Or they didn't say, "You need to be more religious."

Instead, their response was concise and clear. Paul and Silas said, "Believe in the Lord Jesus, and you will be saved—you and your household."[2]

That night the jailer and all his family heard the good news from Paul and Silas. His whole family believed and all were baptized. The jailer's life was completely transformed from one of fear to one of joy. He "was filled with joy because he had come to believe in God—he and his whole family."[3]

The jailer became joyful when he believed in God and had newfound faith. Do you find that you are joyful since believing in God?

Some people say Jesus is dead. They do not believe he is risen. If Jesus is dead, his name would have no power. But he is alive, and his name does have power. Acts 4:12 says, "Salvation is found in no one else, for there is no other name under heaven given to men by which we must be saved."

When we are truly sorry for sinning against God, we repent. We change our way of thinking and divert from our sinful ways.

When we come to the end of ourselves and of our own strength, we realize we can no longer carry the weight of our guilt and our sins. The Holy Spirit comes to convict everyone of individual sin. The Counselor brings humility to the heart.

We rest completely on Jesus Christ. We give ourselves wholeheartedly by faith to the One who carried all our wrongs and transgressions to the cross at Calvary. Jesus, the Passover Lamb without blemish, took upon himself all of our iniquities. In agony, Jesus paid it all.

It is through the grace of God that we are saved. We are not saved because of who we are or what we have done. Salvation cannot be earned. It is not based on merit. We are saved only on the basis of the work of Christ. We are made righteous through him.

Paul described the gospel of Christ as being "the power of God for the salvation of everyone who believes."[4] The term *salvation* signifies a sense of urgency and danger.

Paul explained that salvation "rescued us from the dominion of darkness and brought us into the kingdom of the Son [God] loves."[5] Paul asked, "Who will rescue me from this body of death? Thanks be to God—through Jesus Christ our Lord!"[6] We are made righteous through his work. No longer condemned as sinners, we are set free. God rescued us from darkness, bringing light, comfort, and joy.

The Bible addresses the importance of our confessing Jesus as Lord or putting ourselves under his supreme authority. Paul said, "If you confess with your mouth, 'Jesus is Lord,' and believe in your heart that God raised him from the dead, you will be saved."[7]

Jesus promised us that when we believe in him as our Savior, our lives here on earth are changed. "If anyone is in Christ, he is a new creation; the old has gone, the new has come!"[8]

We now live to please and honor God. And we have eternal life. John 3:15 says, "Everyone who believes in [Jesus] may have eternal life."

When we accept Jesus as our Savior, we obey him and continue in his love. Jesus said, "If you obey my commands, you will remain in my love, just as I have obeyed my Father's commands and remain in his love. I have told you this so that my joy may be in you and that your joy may be complete."[9]

When we accept Jesus Christ into our lives, it is not the end of our spiritual experience with him. Rather, it is the beginning of many great things to come.

Nicodemus, a Pharisee and a member of the Jewish Sanhedrin, met privately with Jesus one night. As a respected interpreter of the law, Nicodemus recognized Jesus' teachings and words. He knew Jesus was a rabbi and a teacher who was sent from God. Then Jesus told Nicodemus, "No one can see the kingdom of God unless he is born again."[10] He needed to receive new life, a second birth.

F. B. Meyer explained the act of being born again, speaking of the second birth: "If you will unite yourself with Jesus Christ who died for us, if you will lift your heart to Him now and say, 'Jesus, I come to Thee, and trust Thee as my Savior,' . . . you do it by an act of your will, you choose Christ. The moment you do that, the Holy Spirit of God binds you in a living union with Christ, and the germ of a new life is put into your soul. You are *born again*! It will begin to work. . . . It will begin to work instantaneously, and you will belong to the aristocracy of the universe, Jesus Christ and the new humanity."[11]

It is clear that the message of Jesus and his disciples was not only of the pardoning of our sins. It also carried with it a reality of a whole new life. Jesus rose from the grave—he could not be defeated by the killing of his body.

Sometimes people's view of God is affected by the lies of the enemy. The enemy will cause people to doubt the truth of the resurrection of Jesus Christ.

Jesus Christ died, was buried, and rose again on the third day. His apostles wrote eyewitness accounts of Christ's resurrection. All of his disciples and Paul heard and saw the risen Christ. He was seen by more than five hundred people at once.

That which the prophets and Jesus had talked about and predicted would happen did come to pass. The early disciples could not help but share the transforming good news they had all witnessed. Jesus is alive! He offers new life to all.

In the end we need to recognize the reality—we are living by faith. We have an open invitation to come to God through Jesus Christ. He is our living High Priest. Christ lives and intercedes for us. We can have access to God every moment of the day. If we haven't accepted his gracious invitation yet, it's not too late.

Prayer
Lord, thank you for sending your Son Jesus. Thank you for the newness of life which comes from forgiveness of sins. Show me any ways I may have hindered my fellowship with you. Forgive me. Restore my relationship with you. Amen.

Scripture for Further Meditation
Matthew 1:21; John 5:24; Romans 1:16; Ephesians 1:13; Titus 3:5–7; 1 John 5:11–12

Takeaway
When you accept God and believe in Jesus Christ, God's Son, you have new life and victory.

PART TWO
Trust in Him

CHAPTER 4

Be a Wise Person

"Everyone who hears these words of mine and puts them into practice
is like a wise man who built his house on the rock."

MATTHEW 7:24

During Jesus' public ministry many people followed him. The reasons for wanting to be near him were many.

Within the crowds were the curious, the ones who had heard of this man and who wanted to find out more about him. There were the needy people who were hoping for some help or even a glimpse of this man. Maybe he would be the answer to their heartaches and problems. There also were the disciples of Jesus, who wanted to learn more about this rabbi. He taught with authority and power.

The crowds seeking him heard the good news of the kingdom. They heard it in the synagogues, in their towns, and throughout the region.

In the Sermon on the Mount, Jesus presented a fresh view of life and customs to his followers. The teachings contained the Lord's Prayer and the Golden Rule. They included the topics of the Beatitudes, legalistic interpretations, and ways to seek God and his righteousness. In the long discourse on the mount, Jesus contrasted his teaching with the Law of Moses. Many of the people were already familiar with the Mosaic Law. He explained how the truths he taught completed and complemented the Old Testament law. He discussed the importance of living authentically,not for appearances only.

At the end of his mountainside sermon in Matthew 7, Jesus told his followers a parable that would apply directly to them. They were the ones who heard his words when he taught the law. He told the parable of the wise and foolish builders.

Jesus explained that whoever hears the words of God and obeys them is wise, similar to a person who builds a house on the rock. When the heavy rains come and strong winds beat against the house, it will stand firm.

In contrast, whoever hears God's words and his instructions and ignores them is foolish. He is like someone who builds his house on the sand. When the floods and gales of wind come, the house will collapse.

The parable is about setting a foundation. It refers to two kinds of people. There are people who make a decision to follow Jesus and become his disciples. And there are those who do not choose to follow him.

Jesus gives everyone an ultimatum of building lives on the rock or the sand. The choices individuals make determine the framework and composition of their lives. It is up to each person to choose to make a foundation, either secure or insecure. The tempests of life will come with their forces of rain and winds. The storms of life will come to the faithful and to the unfaithful.

Storms reveal the foundation upon which we build our lives. Would you say your spiritual foundation is solid or shaky?

When we choose to follow God's instruction, our foundation will be firm and stable. When our foundation is built on God's truths and promises, we know our foundation will be secure. It's an everlasting foundation.

The writer of Proverbs offers words of advice on building with a solid foundation. He says, "By wisdom a house is built, and through understanding it is established."[1] Speaking of wisdom he says, "Get wisdom, get understanding; do not forget my words or swerve from them. Do not forsake wisdom, and she will protect you; love her, and she will watch over you."[2] He emphasizes that people who have a respect for God and who embrace wisdom will be blessed.

James also reminds us of the benefits of obeying God. "The man who looks intently into the perfect law that gives freedom, and continues to do this, not forgetting what he has heard, but doing it—he will be blessed in what he does."[3]

We have been saved through faith. As Christians, faith is our foundation. We know that a house with a strong foundation will stand. Likewise, we have confidence that we will stand firm because of our faith.

Jesus calls us to make a life commitment to him. "Christ's love compels us. . . . And he died for all, that those who live should no longer live for themselves but for him who died for them and was raised again."[4] He gave his life for us, so why wouldn't we give our lives to him? When we trust in Christ alone, the change in our lives is a work of God.

The writer of Hebrews wrote of true Bible faith. He says, "Now faith is being sure of what we hope for and certain of what we do not see."[5] Our faith as believers gives us confidence we will experience what is promised. God gives us an inward conviction that what he has promised, he will deliver. He will keep his word. Faith helps us understand what God has done, what he is doing, and what he will do in the future. He promises to direct our paths when we rely on him. God is always with us and he will cause us to stand.

There's a story about a king who went to a man who was a favorite of his. He told him, "Ask for what you want and I will give it to you."

The man thought, *If I ask to be made general I will readily obtain it. If I ask for half the kingdom he will give it to me. I will ask for something to which all these things will be added.*

So he said to the king, "Give me your daughter so she can be my wife." He knew this made him heir to all the wealth and honors of the kingdom.

In the same way choosing Christ makes us heirs to all the wealth and glory of the Father's kingdom. We shape our future by the choices we make. Our most important choice is whether we will trust in Jesus Christ alone for a new life.

What reasons do you have for following Jesus?

When we are believers and disciples of Jesus, we are no longer on shaky ground. And when our foundation is strong and firm, it is lasting. Are we satisfied to be hearers only of the Word of God? Or do we want to show our commitment to him by acting in obedience?

Considering where you are now in your life, what can you do to be a wise builder? We build not only for today. We build for our future, for our eternity.

Prayer

Sovereign God, thank you for your Word and precepts, giving me a firm foundation. Give me strength when I am weak in spirit, helping me to obey you. Amen.

Scripture for Further Meditation

2 Samuel 22:2; Proverbs 3:10–18; Proverbs 4:10–13; James 3:17

Takeaway

When you trust in God, you can build a strong and secure foundation on his Word and promises.

CHAPTER 5

He Calms Life's Storms

"Keep calm and don't be afraid."

ISAIAH 7:4

When something unexpected happens in your life, how do you deal with it? Are you calm, cool, and collected? Or do you begin to worry and fret?

We all make plans for the future. These plans may relate to family, education, or employment. Generally, we are cognizant of what we would like to see happen in our lives.

As we look optimistically forward to the future, we also know that life can be unpredictable. We cannot be certain what may happen in a week, a month, or even a year. Unpredictable circumstances can wreak havoc amidst beautifully made plans. What we were certain of yesterday, we can no longer be sure of today.

When troubles come, fear can creep into our daily lives. These fears can increase, sometimes taking over our lives. They keep us from the peace we desire.

God is well aware of thefears that arise in our lives. Fear is an inherent weakness that comes and puts blinders on us. Fear puts obstacles and doubts in our way. It holds us back from living a victorious life. There's a saying that goes like this: "Fear is like sand in the machinery of life—faith is like oil."

We read the story in Matthew 8 about Jesus calming a big storm. Not long after Jesus gave his long Sermon on the Mount, he departed from the crowds. In the evening Jesus got into a boat with some of his disciples. They set out to cross to the other side of the Sea of Galilee. Jesus fell asleep in the boat as it moved swiftly ahead. Suddenly a turbulent storm came about on the lake, causing the waves to crash over the boat.

Yet Jesus continued to sleep. Afraid and feeling helpless, the disciples woke him. They said, "Lord, save us! We're going to drown!" He replied, "You of little faith, why are you so afraid?"[1]

Then he stood and spoke to the winds and the waves, reprimanding them. The lake became quiet and serene.

The disciples were astonished that the winds and waves were obedient to the words of Jesus. Yes, it was a miracle. Jesus stilled the storm surrounding the boat.

What we often miss in this story is that Jesus slept peacefully in the midst of the storm. His words to the disciples showed his concern of their unbelief. Although they had been at his side as he taught, they showed fear and unbelief.

His disciples had seen God's power demonstrated in many ways. Yet, they showed their unbelief by being afraid. They wondered if Jesus really cared about them.

Jesus stills the storms of his followers. There are storms of worry and unrest. Even though it may seem that Jesus is not aware of the storms raging in our lives, he is with us. He does know, and he does care about us. He offers peace.

Years ago it was foretold that a child would be born "and he [would] be called . . . Prince of Peace."[2] This child grew to be a man, the One who brings peace.

Jesus told his disciples, "Peace I leave with you; my peace I give you. I do not give to you as the world gives. Do not let your hearts be troubled and do not be afraid."[3] He gives peace to the ones who love him and obey him.

Peace is a result of justification, a result of being made right with God through Jesus Christ. The fruit of righteousness, peace brings quietness and assurance that lasts forever. Paul says the gospel is "the gospel of peace."[4] People who choose to ignore God and his commands miss out on this great peace.

Its flow is unending, like a river. When we are worried, we tend to block that flow, blocking the supply of serenity that can be ours. How do you describe God's peace?

When we are fearful, we're not freely accepting God's supply of assurance that is ours to take. Jesus told his disciples to have faith in God in the midst of life's circumstances. To have faith in God means to count on God to be faithful to us. He will help us release our worries to him. When we are fearful, we can tell him, "Lord, my concerns are in your hands. The rest is up to you."

No matter what our situation, we can know with a deep conviction that we will not be abandoned. Even King David, a man with discouragements and victories, knew he would not be forsaken. He stated, "I was young and now I am old, yet I have never seen the righteous forsaken or their children begging bread."[5] The ones who do right will be taken care of.

We can direct our thoughts to Bible verses when we feel fear and apprehension. The hearing of God's Word produces faith. "Faith comes from hearing the message, and the message is heard through the word of Christ."[6]

We can also meditate on the Scriptures. We can begin with these:

I will lie down and sleep in peace,
    for you alone, O Lord,
    make me dwell in safety.[7]

Those who know your name will trust in you,
    for you, Lord, have never forsaken those who seek you.[8]

You will keep in perfect peace
    him whose mind is steadfast,
    because he trusts in you.[9]

[Jesus said,] "Do not let your hearts be troubled.
    Trust in God; trust also in me."[10]

When the storms darken your life, does it seem like the Son of God is sleeping? Or does he seem near to you?

When we go through the storms of life, God is still with us. Though troubles and challenges come our way, our loving Father will give us what we need to get through them. This is what he promised us: "Never will I leave you; never will I forsake you."[11] We know he will comfort and sustain us. We can count on his faithfulness.

I cannot always trace the onward course
My ship must take,
But looking backward, I behold afar
Its shining wake
Illumined with God's light of love;
And so I onward go
In perfect trust that He who holds
The helm, the course must know.[12]

Prayer
Almighty God, deliver me from the worries and fears of life.
I know you are not far from me. You are near and you care for me.
Bring me peace. Amen.

Scripture for Further Meditation
Psalm 37:5–6; Matthew 6:28–30; Romans 15:13; Hebrews 13:5

Takeaway
When you trust in God, you can count on him to be faithful to you.

CHAPTER 6

Know That He Is God

"Be still, and know that I am God;
I will be exalted among the nations,
I will be exalted in the earth."

PSALM 46:10

Reflect for a moment. What times of quietness do you value most?
Do you take time for quietude in your life?

Throughout the day I like to find times of peace and silence. It
is a time to reflect and rest. It's a time to create. It's also a time to remember my Creator, when I can read from his Word and pray.

When I travel I like to find new places where I can enjoy God's
creation all around me. A few years ago when our family was vaca-
tioning in Florida, I took notes of the sounds around me. I sat outside alone and listened. The palm leaves rustled gently in the breeze.
There were chirping crickets and croaking frogs. Seagulls called out
in the distance. I heard the voices of people walking by. *In our busy
lives, how often do we take the time to be quiet and still?* I thought.

Be still. For some people stillness may be easy to achieve. For
others the mere thought of holding still and being quiet can make
them uncomfortable. Yet, we must not dismiss the importance of
calming ourselves and focusing on our Creator if we desire to commune with him.

In Psalms David spoke of spending time alone with God. He
waited with expectation and confidence. He stated, "Be still before
the LORD and wait patiently for him,"[1] and "My soul finds rest in God

alone; my salvation comes from him."[2] He said, "Many, O Lord my God, are the wonders you have done. The things you planned for us no one can recount to you; were I to speak and tell of them, they would be too many to declare."[3] David was fully aware that God was the Omnipresent One. David praised God for the many wonderful things he had done and for all his wondrous plans for us.

Jesus is an example for us, for he spent time alone with his Father. After Jesus had ministered to crowds of people, he departed to a solitary place. In Mark 1:35 we read he would pray early in the morning. Finding it necessary to retreat to a tranquil place, he often went to the mountains or the seaside. Jesus, our Advocate and Deliverer, continually communed with his heavenly Father. He gained the sustenance and strength he needed.

If Jesus needed to have time of solitude with his Father, how much more must we need to spend time alone with him.

When you need private prayer time, where do you go? What do you do to remove distractions?

For some of us quietness comes naturally in our lives. For others, serenity can be uncomfortable and uneasy.

As we become silent, we have two aims. First, it is important to remove distractions. Life can be fast-paced. We may be overwhelmed with busyness and activities. We may feel we can't slow down. Our busyness can get in the way of having time alone. Find a specific time and place for solitude. Turn off any distracting noise in the background. Take the time to experience God's presence.

Second, besides removing outside distractions, it is essential to silence our inner being. That is, banish all the thoughts within us that pull our attention away. If something needs to be taken care of later, write it down and then forget about it for now.

The pressures of life too easily divert our attention from focusing on the things of God. Tune out the inner noise of worries and distractions. Tune out the inner cacophony of diversions.

We not only seek to be still, but we also want to know him better. "Be still, and *know* that I am God," he said.[4] By quieting ourselves, our body and mind, we can better commune with him. We become tranquil because we can sense God is near. His promptings are gentle.

Be receptive to him, willing to listen. He speaks to us by his Holy Spirit. We learn of his righteous ways. We receive his assurance of how he wants us to live. "I will instruct you and teach you in the way you should go; I will counsel you and watch over you."[5]

When we prepare our heart, we may need to examine our inner attitudes that hinder our prayers. The psalmist David said, "If I had cherished sin in my heart, the Lord would not have listened; but God has surely listened and heard my voice in prayer."[6]

Could it be that our prayers are empty and lifeless because of our disobedience? Or maybe there are bitter or resentful feelings toward others. Quietly, God shows us where we have been found lacking in our Christian walk. We humbly confess our sins to him.

For us to grow and mature as Christian disciples, we must set aside time regularly for prayer and reflection. Let's examine our daily and weekly routine. Look for habits that waste time and habits that don't help our intentions.

Which of the following gets in the way of having our personal devotional and prayer time? Is it setting aside time, being consistent, finding a quiet place, or another obstacle?

When we commit to change our routine and take time to sit in silence before God, we will grow to be more spiritually mature believers.

In silence, we are nourished as we read and meditate on God's Word. In silence, we begin to understand the depth of God's love. Consider these attributes:

Our God is:

- ✦ Creator God
- ✦ God of All Power and Wisdom
- ✦ All-Wise and All-Knowing God
- ✦ God of Tranquility
- ✦ God of Love and Grace

Our God is the God of Abraham, Isaac, and Jacob. Our God is the God of Israel. He is our deliverer. There is no one like him. "I, even I, am the Lord, and apart from me there is no savior. I have revealed and saved and proclaimed."[7]

God is our peace, our shalom. The priestly blessing God gave to Moses for his people is powerful. We can ask for God's blessing as we read the words:

> The Lord bless you
> and keep you;
> the Lord make his face shine upon you
> and be gracious to you;
> the Lord turn his face toward you
> and give you peace.[8]

Feel the Father's love. He loves us with an everlasting love. The Lord alone will be exalted in the earth.

As we are still and quiet we are ready to learn of him. We want to know him better. He is the Almighty God.

Prayer
Awesome God, thank you for your continual presence. You, alone, deserve my praise and adoration. In times of quietude speak to me. Teach me to listen to your still, small voice. Grant me experiential knowledge of you. Amen.

Scripture for Further Meditation
Isaiah 2:11, 17; Isaiah 30:15; Colossians 4:2; Revelation 3:20

Takeaway
When you trust in God, he will reveal himself to you.

CHAPTER 7

Trust in the Potter

"O Lord, you are our Father.
We are the clay, you are the potter;
we are all the work of your hand."

ISAIAH 64:8

I wonder how much time we've spent thinking about the word *trust*. If we didn't trust anyone or anything, we probably wouldn't want to get off the sofa.

I am reminded of a family vacation when I was a child living in Brazil. Our family of five went on an adventurous camping trip at a state park. For me, part of the adventure was learning more about trust.

The park was heavily wooded and had deep gorges. There were rope bridges over the deep gorges. Getting the courage to cross the rope bridges was no small feat. I had to trust that simple bridge to get me across to the other side.

In the same way I trust the rope bridge to carry me, I need to trust my Creator. Then again, considering how great and marvelous our Creator is, I must trust him even more than the rope bridge.

In Genesis, the book of beginnings, we read the announcement—God created. In the beginning he created the universe. He formed the earth and the heavens, with all of their beauty and grandeur.

Then the Lord God made man. He formed Adam "from the dust of the ground and breathed into his nostrils the breath of life, and the man became a living being."[1] Imagine this wonderful miracle of life taking place. This Master Artist is our Creator.

In the Bible our Creator is likened to the Master Potter. The potter forms the clay into pottery, earthenware, and vessels.

In Isaiah, our Creator warned those who defiantly attempt to question him. He said, "Woe to him who quarrels with his Maker. . . . Does the clay say to the potter, 'What are you making?' Does your work say, 'He has no hands'?"[2] Isaiah described words of aggression against God's skills and competence. These words show an attitude of insolence. Yet, our Maker does as he wishes.

The prophet Jeremiah referred to the potter forming a different pot from the same clay. Jeremiah said, "The pot he was shaping from the clay was marred in his hands; so the potter formed it into another pot, shaping it as seemed best to him."[3] The potter made the pot again. He took the marred piece of clay and formed it into a vessel even better, even more beautiful in his eyes.

God can take the irregular parts of our life and with his caring touch mold us into the people he knows we can be. When we are willing, our loving Creator works with us, perfecting us.

The apostle Paul is an example of someone who was molded into a better vessel when God transformed his life completely. You will find the story of Saul's conversion in Acts nine.

In his earlier days, he thought his cause was to persecute and arrest the Lord's disciples. As Saul, he had been known by many people to do great harm to the believers in Jerusalem. Then he had a life-altering journey on his way to Damascus. A bright light from heaven blinded him. Jesus reprimanded Saul for persecuting him.

When Saul was still blind God sent a man named Ananias to visit him and to restore his sight. In a vision the Lord told Ananias that Saul was his chosen vessel who would take his name to the Gentiles and their kings and to the Jews. Saul was given a second chance.

Saul became a changed man and his name was changed to Paul. With a new life and a new mission, he would teach the good news wherever he went. He would teach that Jesus was the Son of God.

Paul referred to the concept of the potter when he wrote to the believers in Rome. Some of the believers had questions about God. Had God forgotten the Jewish people and his promises made to them? Had he given up on them?

Paul spoke on God's sovereignty. He answered, "Who are you, O man, to talk back to God? Shall what is formed say to him who formed it, 'Why did you make me like this?' Does not the potter have the right to make out of the same lump of clay some pottery for noble purposes and some for common use? . . . What if he did this to make the riches of his glory known to the objects of his mercy, whom he prepared in advance for glory—even us, whom he also called?"[4]

When Paul wrote to the church of Galatia, he feared the people were rejecting the faith they once had embraced with joy. He saw them turning from the truths he had taught them. He longed for the time when they would understand fully the gospel of grace.

Paul observed the Galatians drifting back to their old ways. He admonished them, "Are you so foolish? After beginning with the Spirit, are you now trying to attain your goal by human effort?"[5] He said it is the work of the Holy Spirit who changes us.

Speaking to the believers, Paul longed for the time when "Christ is formed in you."[6] In this passage, the word *Christ* refers to "the Christian disposition arising from a sound Christian faith." The term *formed* means "to form or fashion, originally of artists who shape their material into an image." In this verse, *formed* is used to describe the Christian as a child who needs to mature.

Paul explained this forming process. In 2 Corinthians he stated, "As the Spirit of the Lord works within us, we become more and more like him."[7] Paul saw believers as common clay pots who were filled with the light of the gospel. He said, "But we have this treasure in jars of clay to show that this all-surpassing power is from God and not from us."[8] He is working in us and forming us into the image and person he wants us to become.

Some of us have come to him with the broken pieces of our lives. We may not know what God can reshape out of the broken pieces until we give them to him. We can allow him to work in our lives and be our Lord. Have you noticed the ways God is molding you into the person he wants you to be?

Our Maker wants clean jars of clay. Paul wrote to Timothy about staying away from sinful living. He said, "If anyone cleanses himself from these things, he will be a vessel for honor, sanctified, useful to the Master, prepared for every good work."[9] As his vessels, we are useful to accomplish varied tasks.

God wants to design and fashion us to have the likeness of Christ. "Being confident of this, that he who began a good work in you will carry it on to completion until the day of Christ Jesus."[10] Our Maker knows who we are. He also knows who we can become.

God wants to use us—earthen vessels and unique jars of clay. God uses each of us with our own distinctive abilities. In what ways are you using your abilities and gifts?

It has been said that a good deal of talent is lost for the lack of a little courage. To serve him, we must put our confidence in him and not in ourselves. We can put our life into the hands of the Potter. He rewards our faithfulness to him as we use the abilities and gifts with which we have been entrusted.

We can trust our Maker, knowing we can yield to him and allow him to use us as his lovely vessels.

Prayer

All-knowing God, I praise you for being the Divine Creator,
the Master Potter. Thank you that I am wonderfully made.
I am a common clay pot, but also your chosen vessel.
Help me be a vessel that is useful to you. Amen.

Scripture for Further Meditation

Isaiah 29:15–16; Isaiah 45:5; Daniel 4:37; Amos 4:13;
Ephesians 2:10

Takeaway

When you trust in God, you have the good news
and God's all-surpassing power in your life.

PART THREE
Be Transformed by Him

CHAPTER 8

God's Gift of Love

"God has poured out his love into our hearts
by the Holy Spirit, whom he has given us."

ROMANS 5:5

I *love* this ice cream.

I *love* my new car.

I think I *love* her.

Our society gives people a distorted view of love. People are likely to learn what love is through the media and from people around them. From observation, they may get the idea that love is temporary, or it is all about feelings, or it is contingent upon certain factors. When you were a teenager, did your favorite love songs accurately describe love?

To learn what love really is, we must focus on God and his example. What does God's love look like? First Corinthians describes God's kind of love.

> Love is patient, love is kind. It does not envy, it does not boast, it is not proud. It is not rude, it is not self-seeking, it is not easily angered, it keeps no record of wrongs. Love does not delight in evil but rejoices with the truth. It always protects, always trusts, always hopes, always perseveres.
>
> Love never fails.[1]

When I attended a couples' Bible study, the lesson on love was based on these verses in 1 Corinthians. Our teacher did not ask for anyone to comment. But by the end of our time together, all the couples in attendance had shared how they had fallen short of God's kind of love. All had started out with good intentions.

One person told that she chose this passage for her wedding ceremony. The words were beautiful and added something special to the wedding. But it didn't take long after the wedding for her husband and her to forget some of the words. "We should have read these verses again and again," she said. "Our self-seeking ways tend to show how loving we truly are."

Looking at how perfect love is described in 1 Corinthians 13:4–7, which areas could you work on?

Love is a gift of God. It is a sign of the new birth, a proof of salvation. As we live a new life, it is one of the fruits manifested by all who are children of God. The apostle John said, "We know that we have passed from death to life, because we love our brothers."[2] When we are not connected to the source of love, we cannot love as God loves us.

When we receive new life through Christ, it is accompanied by love. This love is evidence that we have been born again. It is the fruit of the Holy Spirit.

John mentions this same kind of love again. "We love because he first loved us."[3] This is *agape* love, which is the ultimate expression of love. *Agape* love connotes "the preciousness or worthiness of the one loved."[4] Since we were reconciled to God through his Son, we can love others as God loves us. It does not come from within us naturally.

Undeniably, it is God who brings about a real change in our lives. It is the power of God that brings about a transformation, enabling us to show love. When we demonstrate his *agape* love we show we are children of God. We will naturally show love to others.

Our love for others will grow as we develop a closer relationship with God. We will desire to learn more of God's Word. Increasingly, we will focus on understanding his ways and will seek to obey him.

Our faith in God expresses itself through love. Love shows consideration for others in deeds. It is evident in our everyday actions.

We must reject and abandon the old ways of our former lifestyle. Peter named things that showed a lack of genuine love. He said to get rid of "all malice and all deceit, hypocrisy, envy, and slander of every kind."[5] These characteristics must no longer be evident in our lives. We must set aside devious ways; set aside jealousy and gossip. Instead, we should seek to become mature, no longer conforming to the ways of the world.

I recall a song our youth group often sang. It said that others would know we are Christians by our love. Jesus said, "By this all men will know that you are my disciples, if you love one another."[6] We show *whose* we are by our love. God loves us perfectly. His love continues to be perfected in us.

When we are found to be lacking in love, could it be that we are not in close fellowship with our heavenly Father?

Since we know and experience God's love toward us, we will show God's love to others. Let's make a difference and be determined to walk in love.

Prayer
Loving God, I'm grateful for your gift of love, a gift that's utterly amazing and unending. Take over in the areas of my life where I fall short in showing love to others. Continue to fill me each day with your abounding love. Amen.

Scripture for Further Meditation
John 15:9–10; 1 Corinthians 13:13; 1 Timothy 1:5; Titus 3:4–5; 1 John 4:7

Takeaway
When God transforms you, his love enters your life and you do what is right and good.

CHAPTER 9

Be Equipped with God's Word

"I have hidden your word in my heart
that I might not sin against you."

PSALM 119:11

A few years ago I scattered grass seed on an empty area of our lawn. I began watering the ground so the seeds would grow. Not long after, along came a robin and a finch devouring the seeds. Disappointed, I tossed out even more seeds.

This reminded me of the parable of the sower. Jesus told of the farmer who sowed his seed in four different soils. Some of the seed fell on the hard path, where the birds came and ate it. When explaining the parable Jesus said, "When anyone hears the message about the kingdom and does not understand it, the evil one comes and snatches away what was sown in his heart. This is the seed sown along the path."[1] The enemy wants to take away the Word that was planted in people's hearts.

Hearing the message of the gospel is imperative. Even more imperative is understanding the messages of God's kingdom.

Consider this: How would your life be different if you didn't have access to the Word of God? What do you think are the benefits of knowing his Word?

The Bible isn't just another good book. It is God's inspired, authoritative Word. The apostle Paul said, "All Scripture is God-breathed and is useful for teaching, rebuking, correcting and training in righteousness, so that the man of God may be thoroughly equipped for every good work."[2]

God reveals himself through the Bible. When we read and study the Bible, we gain a deeper understanding of God's ways and his nature. The Word reveals God's mind, heart, and will. If we desire to be committed deeply in our Christian faith, we must not ignore the theological views closely aligned with the teachings in the Bible.

God's Word is unchanging. Man's thoughts and ideas will change, yet we can trust in God's unchanging Word. God's Word is truth. Jesus told the new Jewish converts, "If you hold to my teaching, you are really my disciples. Then you will know the truth, and the truth will set you free."[3]

We grow spiritually mature when we nourish our spiritual lives. After trusting in Jesus Christ as our Savior and choosing to follow him, we are expected to become more like him. The Scriptures challenge us to grow steadfastly, showing progress in obedience and discipline. We must not remain immature, as babies or children. Instead, we must show signs of spiritual growth.

When Paul wrote to the church in Corinth, he addressed its sin and failings. Many of its problems and divisions were caused by the carnal and immature Christians. In a letter he said, "Brothers, I could not address you as spiritual but as worldly—mere infants in Christ. I gave you milk, not solid food, for you were not yet ready for it. Indeed, you are still not ready. You are still worldly. For since there is jealousy and quarreling among you, are you not worldly? Are you not acting like mere men?"[4] Disappointed in the Corinthians, Paul addressed them as "worldly" and "mere infants in Christ."

As a parent would, Paul scolded them for their rebellious actions. He had been in Corinth for eighteen months, teaching them the basics of Christian doctrine and ethics. Yet they continued to act immaturely, being swayed by lawless ones. Paul continued to question them. Had they forgotten they now belonged to God? Surely they knew God's Holy Spirit resided in them. Had Paul not preached these things to them many times?

Paul cautioned another church, Colosse, about being swayed by deceptive philosophy. The first-century town of Colosse was on a main trading route from the East. People with different and mysterious religious ideas passed through this area. Paul was concerned the new Christians would be deceived by the world's philosophies that sounded good. He warned them that they must not be enticed by the world's empty and deceptive philosophy. Why follow shallow philosophy when they have received fullness in Christ?

Paul gave them practical instructions for staying firm in the faith. He said, "So then, just as you received Christ Jesus as Lord, continue to live in him, rooted and built up in him, strengthened in the faith as you were taught, and overflowing with thankfulness."[5] Note that Paul told them to be thankful. Someone who has a thankful heart will not be easily swayed from the fullness Christ provides. A person overflowing with thankfulness will show signs of spiritual progress.

God's Word brings us to a place of spiritual maturity and depth. It is the source of nourishment. Jesus said, "It is written: 'Man does not live on bread alone, but on every word that comes from the mouth of God.'"[6] His Word continually nourishes our soul.

The Word is active. It does not come from men, but from God, the ultimate authority.[7] It is at work in the lives of believers and unbelievers. It will "cut to the heart," convicting people of their sins.[8]

Ephesians 6 reminds us to take hold of the Word of God, which is the sword of the Holy Spirit. As believers we are in God's army. Each of us should be equipped with a sword to fight in the battle against the enemy. We can take it and use it with confidence, knowing it has mighty power.

We can use the sword of the Spirit to defeat the enemy. Jesus was equipped with the sword of the Spirit when he was tempted in the desert. Every time he was tempted he stated, "It is written," quoting Scriptures.[9] Every time he was victorious. We as believers can also say, "It is written," speaking God's Word with authority. God says we need to speak his Word, for God empowers his Word.

To grow strong in our faith we must trust and obey God. But how can we obey him if we do not have a solid grasp of his Word?

We will examine four important ways to grow in biblical knowledge.

Read God's Word

Clearly, if we desire to enjoy a close walk with God, we must know what his guidelines and promises are for us. We become the people we ought to be through the transforming power of his Word.

When we learn more of God's Word, it changes us. We grow spiritually. The writer of Hebrews wrote, "For the word of God is living and active. Sharper than any double-edged sword, it penetrates even to dividing soul and spirit, joints and marrow; it judges the thoughts and attitudes of the heart."[10] The Word of God comes to life and speaks to us. His words can pierce the soul and spirit. They can appraise the heart's desires.

Set aside a devotional time each day to read the Scriptures and pray. Silence the external noise. Find a quiet place. During the years of Jesus' ministry, he rose early in the morning, sought out a quiet place, and prayed. Even though he had a busy schedule, he made time to commune with his Father.

Study God's Word

In Acts 17:11 we read that the Jews of Berea eagerly studied the Scriptures every day. Paul considered them to be an example for others since they carefully examined the Scriptures to see if Silas's and his statements were true. As a result, many Jews and prominent Greeks became believers.

We must not neglect to examine the foundations of our faith. Attend a church that preaches the gospel and the truths of the Bible. Be involved in a church that does not stray from biblical teachings. When we are not deeply rooted in the Word, it is easier to be deceived by false teachers and philosophies.

Take part in small group lessons and discussions. Bible study groups offer informal and interactive study. Participants learn more about God and discuss how they can apply the Word to their lives.

Some Christians neglect to get connected with other believers. They miss out on the benefits of learning from others who have years of Bible knowledge and experiences to share.

Are you growing in Bible knowledge? If not, what steps can you take this week to do so?

Memorize God's Word

King David learned that the solution to combat his wandering ways was to memorize the Word. He desired to follow God wholeheartedly. David said, "I seek you with all my heart; do not let me stray from your commands. I have hidden your word in my heart that I might not sin against you."[11]

When we memorize verses we keep God's thoughts, words, and promises in our minds. We keep front and center our sword to protect us in our spiritual struggles.

Meditate on God's Word

Another way to have a deeper understanding of the Bible is to meditate on it. When we meditate on something, we consider it and ponder it. We reflect on it. As we meditate on God's precepts and directives for living, we learn new truths we had not observed before. We gain new insights into the mysteries of God. If we want to be wise and successful, we need to go to the Word.

When Joshua was Israel's new leader, God spoke to him. God had an important directive for his people that came with a wonderful promise. Joshua said, "Do not let this Book of the Law depart from your mouth; meditate on it day and night, so that you may be careful to do everything in it."[12] The people of Israel were told if they did this, they would prosper and find success.

Do we often examine our innermost thoughts and actions? Paul urged the believers, "Do not conform any longer to the pattern of this world, but be transformed by the renewing of your mind. Then you will be able to test and approve what God's will is—his good, pleasing, and perfect will."[13]

As we feed our new nature with God's thoughts, our lives continue to be transformed. God continues a good work in us.

Prayer

Lord of the Word, thank you for your Word that is a light
for my path. Help me as I apply what I'm learning from the Bible.
You said you would instruct me and teach me in the way
I should go. Amen.

Scripture for Further Meditation

Isaiah 55:11; 1 Thessalonians 2:13; 1 Timothy 4:13; Hebrews 5:11–14;
1 Peter 1:23

Takeaway

When God transforms you, you delight in gaining a deeper
understanding of him and his character through his Word.

CHAPTER 10

Become a New Person

"If anyone is in Christ, he is a new creation;
the old has gone, the new has come!"
2 CORINTHIANS 5:17

There is a story of a Native American tribal leader who became a Christian. A visiting pastor asked him how he was doing as a new Christian. In his simple way the tribal leader explained how he resolves an inner struggle in his life. He said, "I have two dogs living inside me, a good dog and a mean dog. They are always fighting. The good dog wants me to do good things. The mean dog wants me to do bad things. Do you want to know which one wins? It is the one I feed the most!" This man learned he needed to deepen his devotion to what is good. For it is human to do bad things.

Christians have an old nature and a new nature. The old nature is the old self from one's physical birth. It is based on the flesh, and it brings the sinful nature with it. Before trusting Christ, we were children of disobedience, conforming to the things of this world.

The old self is controlled by the flesh. The apostle Paul said, "The man without the Spirit does not accept the things that come from the Spirit of God, for they are foolishness to him, and he cannot understand them, because they are spiritually discerned."[1]

Persons with the old nature have a problem with the heart. Without the Spirit of God, they have a heart that is not open to the ways of God. It is a hardened heart. Causes of a hardened heart are unbelief and sin. They choose not to believe God's truths or listen to his still, quiet voice.

In the book of Jeremiah the words of the Lord say, "The heart is deceitful above all things and beyond cure. Who can understand it?"[2] The heart of sin cannot be cured with one's own efforts. There is no hope with one's own works.

Often what we cannot learn by instruction or principles, we must learn by experience. Some people call these experiences hard knocks. C. S. Lewis eloquently wrote about the pain he experienced. He said, "Pain plants the flag of truth in the mind."

When we get too far in our disobedience, we find it does not pay. Change begins when there is a desire for change. There is a hunger for a better way to live. There is dissatisfaction or frustration that brings a sense of hopelessness to life.

Believers experience a spiritual birth through faith in Jesus Christ. Paul wrote about putting on the character of Christ. We put away the old self with its deeds. We "have put on the new self, which is being renewed in knowledge in the image of its Creator."[3] The new self is controlled by the Holy Spirit.

The disciple John said, "No one who is born of God will continue to sin, because God's seed remains in him; he cannot go on sinning, because he has been born of God."[4] So it is the duty of the believer to live with the new nature in control, not to make room for sin in one's life.

Having received a spiritual birth, there is a change in the believer's life. With a new life, we are cleansed from sins that bind us to the old nature. We are freed from harmful attitudes and habits that weigh us down and hold us back from receiving all God has for us.

When we ask God to make us new, he removes our sins and we begin new lives. It is as though the dead leaves of a tree are removed. There is a new season ahead. The buds of a new season are forming. There is a new future and a new freedom not known before. When there is a changed heart, there is a changed life.

Spiritual transformation is a work of God. It is the process of becoming more like Jesus. We are surrendered and yielded to him. As he changes the heart and changes one's attitudes and actions, we are more aware of his presence in our lives.

The new birth gives us a new nature. We escape the corruption of the world's ways. Taking part in the divine nature, we show his nature in our living.

When God changes our hearts he changes our thinking. In Romans, Paul said not to be conformed to worldly patterns, "but be transformed by the renewing of your mind."[5] This process of renewing is a continual process. He reminded new believers of the teachings "to put off your old self . . . to be made new in the attitude of your minds; and to put on the new self, created to be like God in true righteousness and holiness."[6] Paul told the believers that since they had a different heart, their actions must also be different. He added, "Get rid of all bitterness, rage and anger, brawling and slander, along with every form of malice. Be kind and compassionate to one another, forgiving each other, just as in Christ God forgave you."[7]

When we are reborn into the family of God, we will feed the new nature with that which pleases God. We know the importance of spending more time in the Word, storing it in the mind and heart. When we read the Word, God is working in our life and changing us.

God shows us what we need to know about ourselves and about him. He gives us discipline and self-control. As believers we do not continue doing what we used to do, for we are no longer slaves to sin.

What are some changes God has made in your life since you've become a Christian? What part of the old nature do you still need to remove?

As we are rooted in righteousness and grounded in his Word, we will grow in our faith. We have the Word of God and the Spirit of God to empower and help us. We have a new heart and a new nature.

Reflect upon the changes God has made in your life. Thank him for the ways he has transformed your life.

Prayer

Dear Father, thank you for all you have given me through your Son. Thank you for a new way of life. Continue to work in me. Amen.

Scripture for Further Meditation

John 6:63; Romans 6:6; 2 Corinthians 3:18, 2 Corinthians 5:14–15; Galatians 2:20

Takeaway

When God transforms you, a spiritual birth has taken place, bringing a changed heart and a new nature.

CHAPTER 11

Have a Temperate Nature

"Everyone should be quick to listen, slow to speak
and slow to become angry."

JAMES 1:19

This verse sounds like a proverb. In fact, the book of James is some-times called the Proverbs of the New Testament. It reads like a trea-sure trove of concise and significant proverbs for successful living. The book of James is traditionally thought to be written by James, the half-brother of Jesus. Directed to new believers, James describes Christianity in action. He explains how to live right, applying the Christian faith to everyday situations.

James 1:19 reminds us to be attentive listeners. This is an action vital to having healthy relationships with others. It is also vital in hav-ing a genuine relationship with God. As attentive listeners, we focus on the speaker and what is being said. We seek to tune out distrac-tions so we can be more attuned to the messenger and the message.

If we listen attentively, we are less likely to be thinking of a reply while the other person speaks. We are not likely to interrupt or re-spond quickly with our judgments and opinions.

Can you name a time when you wish you had been quick to lis-ten and slow to speak?

There's a saying, "Discretion in speech is more than eloquence." When we are slow to speak we are able to have a thoughtful and con-siderate response. We have had more time to hear and understand what is said. As a result, we are less likely to act out of anger. It's been said that when we suppress a moment's anger, we may prevent a day of sorrow.

Several of King Solomon's proverbs remind us of the importance of self-control when talking. Note these verses in Proverbs:

A gentle answer turns away wrath,
    but a harsh word stirs up anger.
The tongue of the wise commends knowledge,
    but the mouth of the fool gushes folly.[1]

The tongue that brings healing is a tree of life,
    but a deceitful tongue crushes the spirit.[2]

A hot-tempered man stirs up dissension,
    but a patient man calms a quarrel.[3]

A man finds joy in giving an apt reply—
    and how good is a timely word![4]

What we say has the potential for harm or good. Instead of causing disunity, we must be peace loving. Instead of acting out of selfishness or pride, we must be thoughtful of others. This is shown with a gentle demeanor and awareness of interests of others.

In the book of James, chapter 3, James wrote about the importance of taming the tongue. Although it is a small thing, it can do a lot of damage. The tongue is compared to a tiny spark that can set a great forest on fire. As we know, it can be hard to tame.

James reminds us that true faith is shown to be relevant by our conduct. He says, "Who is wise and understanding among you? Let him show it by his good life, by deeds done in the humility that comes from wisdom."[5] We are considered wise not only by our knowledge, but also by our humble deeds. Jesus is our example of humility. He was meek and not prideful. When we live and act with wisdom from above, we are peaceable and gentle. We are considerate of others.

A pastor told the story of a teenager in his youth group. The young man was a talented musician and a church member. But he seemed to be in the middle of every problem in their youth group. He was always in some kind of trouble.

One summer the teen went to a youth camp. Before he left, the pastor, youth leaders, and church leaders decided to pray for him every day. Then, at one of the youth camp meetings, the teen made an announcement. He told them he had been saved that week! Before that week, he had professed to be a Christian. But he was living a counterfeit life. He did not have Christ in his life and had not repented of his sins.

The pastor happily reported that there was a dramatic change in the teen's life. Now a genuine Christian, the teen was serving God faithfully with a changed heart and a change in conduct.

Having theological knowledge alone is not sufficient. One must make a decision to truly repent and trust in Jesus Christ to be Lord and Savior. This brings about a changed life.

David asked the Lord to keep him from willful sins. He desired to live in the fear of the Lord, with reverence and trust. David said, "May the words of my mouth and the meditation of my heart be pleasing in your sight, O Lord, my Rock and my Redeemer."[6] With a meek spirit, he sought to speak the words which please the Redeemer.

There is a saying, "It's good to be saved and know it, but it's better to be saved and show it." Does your life display temperate conduct? Are there any areas to work on?

Our faith must affect how we speak and respond to others. The grace of God in our hearts should cause us to be controlled and peace loving.

Prayer
Lord, help me guard what I say. Help me to be a
peace-loving person. Thank you for your wisdom, enabling me
to live a self-controlled life. Amen.

Scripture for Further Meditation
Psalm 18:21; Psalm 34:12–14; Proverbs 25:11; Ephesians 4:29; Titus 2:11–12

Takeaway
When God transforms you, you live in harmony with one another.

PART FOUR
Abide in Him

CHAPTER 12

Live a Blessed Life

"But his delight is in the law of the LORD,
and on his law he meditates day and night.
He is like a tree planted by streams of water,
which yields its fruit in season
and whose leaf does not wither.
Whatever he does prospers."

PSALM 1:2–3

I sat under a large, full-grown maple tree on the bank of a lake. Its wide-reaching branches with deep green foliage provided ample shade. It was a welcoming place of rest and refreshment.

The expansive roots of the mature tree extended deep and wide. Some of the tree's long roots reached down into the water, drinking incessantly from its source of life. Other roots stretched out deep into the soil surrounding the tree. The tree's good root system enabled it to thrive.

In Psalm 1 David wrote about the person who is blessed. Note three things about this person. First, we observe the close friends he keeps. He "does not walk in the counsel of the wicked or stand in the way of sinners or sit in the seat of mockers."[1] Take note of the kind of company we keep. Do we walk with friends who offer bad advice, or stand with ones who continually sin? Do we sit with friends who scoff at the things of God? Look out for the spiritual snares.

Second, we observe the reading and thinking of the blessed person. David said, "His delight is in the law of the LORD, and on his law he meditates day and night."[2] Do we spend time reading and listening to God's words and truths? Thinking on Scripture passages helps us understand and apply them.

Third, note that the one who is blessed is fruitful. "He is like a tree planted by streams of water, which yields its fruit in season and whose leaf does not wither. Whatever he does prospers."[3] The fruit is continual and appropriate to the changing seasons. There is growth and sustenance.

Psalm 1 verse 3 compares the righteous believer to a tree. Planted by streams of water, the tree was strong and fruitful season after season. Its leaves were fresh and green, a sign of life. Its roots reached deep, continually getting moisture.

In comparison, the sinners were like a tree withered by drought. "They are like chaff that the wind blows away."[4] Living apart from God, the sinners did not prosper.

The prophet Jeremiah used a similar contrast. He told the people whom to trust. The people who put their trust and confidence in God are blessed.[5] But "cursed is the one who trusts in man, who depends on flesh for his strength and whose heart turns away from the LORD. He will be like a bush in the wastelands; he will not see prosperity when it comes. He will dwell in the parched places of the desert."[6]

The desert tree has shallow roots. It cannot depend on a constant source of water. Its leaves are not always alive with color, and it does not always produce fruit. There may have been blossoms on the tree at one time, but the blossoms wither.

When have you experienced spiritual drought? How did you move on through the dry times?

As believers, we build a deeper root system when we abide in God. We meditate on his Word and gain nourishment from it. Our spiritual formation is like a tree with its roots growing wide and deep, in the rich soil of God's Word. The tree stands strong, established with a solid and firm foundation. When we abide in God it is he who helps us produce the fruit of the Spirit. This fruit is evidence of Christian character. They are: "love, joy, peace, patience, kindness, goodness, faithfulness, gentleness and self-control."[7]

The mature tree extends its fruitfulness to a wide area surrounding it. It bears fruit and spreads forth foliage. A strong and full tree offers shade for all who are nearby. Like a mature tree, the believer is blessed and other people share in the blessings.

What are some blessings God has given you?

God's divine love and grace cause us to live a fruitful and blessed life. The spiritual fruit is the outcome of his presence in our lives. It is the result of his work.

Some Christians try to get results in their own human attempts rather than staying in fellowship with Christ and letting him work and produce the fruit naturally. It is the kind of fruit that comes when we are abiding in Christ, bringing glory to God. "I am the vine; you are the branches. If a man remains in me and I in him, he will bear much fruit; apart from me you can do nothing."[8]

When Paul wrote to the faithful Christians in Ephesus, he spoke of God's riches that also are ours. He said, "I pray that out of [the Father's] glorious riches, he may strengthen you with power through his Spirit in your inner being, so that Christ may dwell in your hearts through faith. And I pray that you, being rooted and established in love, may have power, together with all the saints, to grasp how wide and long and high and deep is the love of Christ."[9]

Who can understand the expanse of his love? Believers have roots reaching into his divine love. And love is the evidence that we are abiding in him.

Prayer
Righteous Lord, thank you that I can put my trust and confidence in you. Equip me with your might and strength. Keep me strong in the faith. Amen.

Scripture for Further Meditation
Psalm 5:11–12; Psalm 119:1–7; John 15:4

Takeaway
When you abide in God by delighting in his instructions, you will be fruitful.

CHAPTER 13

We Are God's Children

"How great is the love the Father has lavished on us,
that we should be called children of God!"

1 JOHN 3:1

Ever since I was a child I knew I was wanted and loved by my father. He let me know I had value and importance to him.

Because my own dad was loving and trustworthy I could easily picture my heavenly Father as a loving and trustworthy Father. One day I understood the message of God's care and compassion for me. Aware of God's mercy and grace, I became his child. He would no longer be someone who seemed distant.

Becoming Children of God

What does it mean to be a child of God? When we were sinners we could not have a real relationship with God. For he is holy. Yet he loved us so much he provided a way that we could have access to him, by sending his Son.

Christ went to the cross and bore upon himself all the sins of mankind. He redeemed us by paying the price for our iniquities, making a way to God. When we admitted and acknowledged our sins to God, he forgave us. We were born again when we put our faith in Christ, becoming God's child. Being instantly adopted into his family, we belong to him. He gave us a divine nature so we can live new and different lives.

The disciple Peter reminded believers of this fact. He said, "His divine power has given us everything we need for life and godliness through our knowledge of him who called us by his own glory and goodness. Through these he has given us his very great and precious promises, so that through them you may participate in the divine nature and escape the corruption in the world caused by evil desires."[1]

Christians partake of the new nature, enabled by the Holy Spirit. New believers take part in *regeneration*, meaning being "born again." They enter a new life in the family of God. John says, "Yet to all who received him, to those who believed in his name, he gave the right to become children of God."[2]

We are stamped with a permanent seal of confirmation that we are, indeed, his. Paul explained this in his letter to the Ephesians. He said, "Having believed, you were marked in him with a seal, the promised Holy Spirit, who is a deposit guaranteeing our inheritance until the redemption of those who are God's possession."[3] After Christ's work on earth was finished and he returned to heaven, he sent a Comforter who was a pledge of our inheritance.

We are born of God and we should have characteristics of our heavenly Father. The apostle Paul reminded believers to imitate God in all we do, because we are his children.

God leads and speaks truth to his children through his Holy Spirit who dwells within us. His Spirit puts to death the sinful nature, thereby causing us to live well. As a loving and caring Father, he shows us the better way. In his letter to the Romans, Paul said, "Those who are led by the Spirit of God are sons of God."[4] How wonderful that through his divine Spirit, God confirms with our spirit that we are, indeed, his children.

Enabled to Call God "Father"

Our Father God has shown his love for us and continues to bestow his love on us. As his children each of us has worth and value to him. God claims us as his own. He says, "You are mine," accepting us as his sons and daughters. What a great privilege.

We are comforted in knowing we are always accepted by our Father. For he says, "Never will I leave you; never will I forsake you."[5] It is reassuring to know that he accepts us unconditionally.

In the letter of 1 John, we read that God's children "have an anointing from the Holy One, and all of [us] know the truth."[6] This anointing shows us the truth. It teaches us about all things, making known to us the truths of spiritual matters. This anointing shows us the true deity of Christ—Jesus Christ is God who has come in the flesh. It causes us to confess our need to trust in Christ alone for a new life and a new nature.

Access to the Father

We have close fellowship with our Father. Since we are his children, we can approach him at any time. We have free access to him. Nothing can keep us away from him.

Christ alone took the penalty for our sins when he died. But he rose from the dead, becoming our advocate. John wrote of the One who stands up for us and defends us. He said, "We have one who speaks to the Father in our defense—Jesus Christ, the Righteous One."[7] How wonderful that Jesus is our supporter and defender when we confess our iniquities and failings to him.

Characteristics of God's Children

How do the children of God live? The letter of 1 John lists what makes us distinct.

- ✧ We do not love the world system around us.
- ✧ We do what is right.
- ✧ We live a righteous life.
- ✧ We are obedient to our Father.
- ✧ We do not continue to sin.
- ✧ We love one another.
- ✧ We love our heavenly Father.
- ✧ We who believe that Jesus is the Son of God have overcome the world.[8]

Inheritance with Christ

As children of God, we express our thankfulness to him for all he has done for us. He has made us his heirs. We are delighted that he has made us eligible to share in the inheritance with other believers. We share in the riches we have inherited.

God promised us eternal life when Christ returns to earth to gather his church. John says, "We know that when [Christ] appears, we shall be like him, for we shall see him as he is."[9] John encourages believers to continue to abide in him "so that when he appears we may be confident and unashamed before him at his coming."[10]

We await with eagerness the day when our Lord Jesus Christ returns and takes us to our heavenly home. We will be like him with glorified bodies. He "will transform our lowly bodies so that they will be like his glorious body."[11]

Paul spoke of the mystery of the resurrected body. He said, "We will not all sleep, but we will all be changed—in a flash, in the twinkling of an eye, at the last trumpet. For the trumpet will sound, the dead will be raised imperishable, and we will be changed."[12] God will receive us joyfully as his beloved children. We will have deeper fellowship with him than we have ever had before. And we will enjoy close fellowship with saved loved ones—family and friends whom we knew on earth.

The amazing fact of Christianity is not solely that Christ died and rose again, but that as God's children, the Christian has a final resurrection. The eternal God, having conquered death, has given the believer eternal life with him.[13] So not only do we have hope in Christ for this life. We also have wonderful hope for a life coeternal with God in heaven, our final home.

He is our God. We are his children. As our Father, he will never turn a deaf ear to our prayers. He has promised a personal and long-lasting relationship with us.

Prayer

Dear Lord, it is with gratitude that I'm able to call you my heavenly Father. Thank you for the pledge of my inheritance, the Comforter, the Holy Spirit. I pray that I will walk worthy as your child. Amen.

Scripture for Further Meditation

Galatians 4:4–7; Ephesians 3:6; Ephesians 5:1–2

Takeaway

When you abide in God as his child, you share in the inheritance with other believers.

CHAPTER 14

Continue in Prayer

"Call to me and I will answer you
and tell you great and unsearchable things
you do not know."

JEREMIAH 33:3

Vonette Bright worked alongside her husband, Bill, for years with Campus Crusade for Christ. The day I met her she was the guest speaker at a luncheon at Taylor University. I looked forward to meeting her and speaking with her. I asked Vonette to sign a book Bill had written.

On the inside of the book cover she wrote Jeremiah 33:3. Then she said, "Just think of this as the phone call verse. When we call to God, he will answer us."

The Bible teaches us prayer is important. The Christian life is not sustainable unless we have prayer and communication with our heavenly Father. Just as breathing is natural to the physical person, prayer is natural to the spiritual person. As we have daily fellowship we will see more of his presence and power in our lives. As we make ourselves available to God, he will work in our lives. Praying to our heavenly Father is a great privilege.

What is prayer? Prayer is spending time in communion with God. It is talking with our heavenly Father and having him speak with us. John Calvin called prayer "the soil of faith."

Prayer is a cry. We are crying out to God. Paul explained, "You received the Spirit of sonship. And by him we cry, '*Abba*, Father.'"[1]

Prayer is a call. The Lord God says, "Call to me and I will answer you and tell you great and unsearchable things you do not know."[2]

Prayer is asking. When Jesus taught about prayer he said, "Ask and it will be given to you; seek and you will find; knock and the door will be opened to you."[3] Jesus also stated, "And I will do whatever you ask in my name, so that the Son may bring glory to the Father."[4]

Why should we pray? It is vital since it is necessary for salvation. "Everyone who calls on the name of the Lord will be saved."[5]

Praying is evidence we are truly believers. It is integral to our new nature. As children of God, praying is an essential way we have a genuine relationship with him. It is expressing our living faith relationship. In the book of Luke Jesus said, "And will not God bring about justice for his chosen ones, who cry out to him day and night? Will he keep putting them off?"[6] God has a father's compassion. Because of man's boldness he answers.

Prayer connects us to a powerful God. It moves the heart of God, bringing us into his holy presence. When we pray and believe, we see God working in our lives. We know he is working in the world as we experience a deeper faith relationship with him. Jesus told his disciples we can pray with confidence.

The writer of Hebrews said, "Let us then approach the throne of grace with confidence, so that we may receive mercy and find grace to help us in our time of need."[7] The power of God and the power of prayer are directly related.

Prayer is an important pillar of spiritual discipline and growth. We are reminded, "Be joyous always; pray continually; give thanks in all circumstances, for this is God's will for you in Christ Jesus."[8]

Prayer keeps us vigilant and on guard against the enemy's wiles. The enemy is "like a roaring lion," a prowler looking to deceive and devour.[9] We must be watchful and alert, not neglecting our prayers.

In the book of Matthew, Jesus provided a model for how his followers should pray. Jesus prayed:

"Our Father in heaven,
hallowed be your name,
your kingdom come,

your will be done
   on earth as it is in heaven.
Give us today our daily bread.
Forgive us our debts,
   as we also have forgiven our debtors.
And lead us not into temptation,
   but deliver us from the evil one."[10]

This prayer is brief and simply stated. There is adoration of God and petition for his will to be accomplished. There is dependence on God for provisions for life. We trust him to provide for our needs. There is dependence on God for pardoning of sin and for overcoming temptation. This prayer shows humility.

Looking at the model prayer of Jesus, how do forgiveness and prayer work together?

Jesus, the sinless Son of God, prayed to his Father. Through his example, he showed us that prayer was vitally important. During his ministry on earth, he often left the crowds of people to be alone and commune with his Father. Given that we are born sinners, how much more should we find prayer important!

Although prayer was natural for Jesus, it was also a necessity for him. It is evident how his everyday life of prayer and his wisdom and power were related. Jesus used prayer to build his kingdom. When he prayed, he asked that God's name be glorified. Jesus had an ongoing sense of expectation that his Father would work through him. With an attitude of expectancy he said, "It is the Father, living in me, who is doing his work."[11]

Prayer was an integral part of the ministry and teachings of Jesus. There are many examples of Jesus naturally praying to God, praising him, and giving thanks.

Jesus prayed before choosing his disciples. One day he went to a mountain to pray, staying all night in prayer. The next morning he asked several of his followers to come with him. Eventually, he chose twelve disciples to be with him, whom he also called his apostles. We know Jesus continued to pray for his disciples. He knew them well, their strengths and failings. Jesus told Simon Peter he prayed for him that his faith would not fail. Jesus also prayed for the believers who would accept the message of the disciples.[12]

Jesus prayed on the day of his death. His prayer was one of compassion for the men who nailed him to the cross. He said, "Father, forgive them, for they do not know what they are doing."[13]

Just as God has done in the past, today God continues to build his kingdom through prayer. He never gives up on any of us. Peter explained, "He is patient with you, not wanting anyone to perish, but everyone to come to repentance."[14] And with the help of his followers he is bringing people to a new relationship with him.

We seek to live peaceful lives. Yet, we cannot know or control all the circumstances in an unpredictable world. We may face some difficult and dark situations. God may have some lessons to teach us from these difficult trials. Consider asking him, "Teach me what you want me to learn."

As you consider your prayers, what concerns take most of your time in prayer?

Let us be persistent and bold when praying. We must not be discouraged by difficulties. Continue to pray, trusting in God for his help.

Throughout the years I have seen God answer the prayers of our family. He healed my mother, sister, and brother who were seriously ill. He has protected us during the many years of travels. I've seen firsthand how my parents, sister, brother, and I were spared from being in several car accidents on two continents. We have been in awe at how God has watched over us. Many times through the years God provided what we needed at the time.

He has protected my own family as we've traveled. For example, one day my children and I narrowly missed being in a car accident by seconds. I was driving to a campground and stopped at the stoplight. When the light turned green I strangely hesitated to go left. I had checked and there were no cars coming from the left or right. Then when I looked left again, I saw a red sports car quickly approaching and speeding through the red light. My children and I just looked at each other in amazement. As we watched the sports car fly past us down the highway, we were so grateful to God for protecting us. We said a prayer of thanksgiving.

As a child of missionaries, I've seen God work in many people's lives. They have been transformed by the redeeming power of God's grace. I know of many instances where God has worked miraculously.

I remember one day when I was a child our family made a home visit in a small town. The people were many kilometers away from any medical help. When we arrived, we met a mother and father who were very distressed. The mother was holding their newborn son who was very ill. The parents had done what they could to help their little baby. They were fearful he would die. The parents didn't know how much longer he would survive. My father lovingly took the baby in his arms and prayed aloud for the little one. He prayed God would heal the little baby. I remember being hopeful about the little boy.

The next time we visited the family we arrived to see a happy mother and father. Their baby had survived. It was so wonderful to visit the family again and see a healthy baby boy. His parents had more great news. They had named their baby *Samuel*, in honor of my father.

One day my mother heard of a teenager, Marcos, who was very ill with a serious heart condition. His brother attended the Bible institute where my father was a professor. My mother was very concerned about this young man's need. She went to the family's home and prayed for Marcos, believing God would heal him.

After the prayer Marcos felt better. When the young man went to see his doctor, the doctor was amazed at what he saw. He said Marcos had been cured of his heart condition and had a clean bill of health. Yes, we can believe in the power of prayer.

How do you feel when a person tells you he or she is praying for you? I know it greatly encourages me. I'm thankful for the prayers of many people, especially of my grandparents. On my thirteenth birthday Grandfather Lehman sent me a very special letter. In it he said he and Grandmother Lehman prayed for me every day.

God hears our prayers. His eyes are on the righteous and his ears are open to our prayers. He is eager to answer them. In his own way and time, he answers. A merciful father of tender compassion, he continually shows his care over us. God delights in the prayers of his children.

Prayer

Father in heaven, you are holy and greatly to be praised. Thank you for the privilege of prayer, that I can come to you with my cares and concerns. Show me my failings and forgive me of my sins. You are the all-powerful God. In Jesus' name. Amen.

Scripture for Further Meditation

Psalm 34:15; Luke 11:5–10; Romans 12:2, 12; Philippians 4:6; Hebrews 10:22

Takeaway

When you abide in God, pray continually, giving thanks. He will answer.

CHAPTER 15

Receive a Triple Blessing

"Grace, mercy and peace from God the Father and Christ Jesus our Lord."

1 TIMOTHY 1:2

Let's consider the words *grace*, *mercy*, and *peace*. How do we receive these qualities? They come from God and his Son, Jesus Christ.

When the apostle Paul wrote to Timothy, he greeted him as a true son in the faith. Paul's salutation held a greeting with a triple blessing for his friend. This blessing was for grace, mercy, and peace.

Grace

Grace is what God gives us, even though we do not deserve it.

We have been saved through grace. But grace was not offered only for this initiatory act. It was extended through God's continual kindness to us. It continues to be a sustaining influence that empowers believers to advance in the Christian life. Paul said, "I do not set aside the grace of God, for if righteousness could be gained through the law, Christ died for nothing![1] We must not abandon the grace of God in our day-to-day lives.

Instead, we will continue to experience and live in his grace. When Paul felt weak and helpless, God reassured him with the words, "My grace is sufficient for you, for my power is made perfect in weakness."[2] Grace is God's empowerment that enables us to do what we cannot do ourselves. It empowers us to overcome sin. It empowers us to live holy lives.

Sue was raised in a Christian family. As a young teen she

wandered from the biblical teachings of her parents. She ran away from home and drifted for years from the Christian foundation of her childhood. Her parents felt pain and sadness.

Then Sue began to realize her sinful ways. She had regret and feelings of unworthiness.

Feeling the weight of guilt, Sue asked a Christian friend, "Is there grace enough for me?"

The good news is that there was and is enough grace. Sue returned to God and left behind her destructive habits. Although Sue knows she can't change what she did in the past, she can move forward and strive to obey God.

Whether we are experiencing new life in Christ or we're longtime believers, all of us can enjoy the abundant riches of his grace. He continues to give freely of his wonderful kindness and favor to us. We can continue to look to God for help. And he will continue to supply his abounding grace in the future.

How has God's grace helped you to rise above your circumstances?

Mercy

Mercy means God does not give us the punishment we deserve.

In Isaiah, God makes an open invitation for all to seek him while he can be found. He invites the wicked to leave their evil ways and thoughts. He asks them to turn to the Lord God, and he will have mercy and will pardon freely.[3]

In the Old Testament book of Micah we see a theme of a just and merciful God. God gives a directive to his people to exemplify their true faith. He says, "And what does the Lord require of you? To act justly and to love mercy and to walk humbly with your God."[4] When we show mercy, we display acts of compassion. Showing mercy, we are more willing to forgive others.

God shows mercy to us through his Son. Peter said, "In his great mercy he has given us new birth into a living hope through the resurrection of Jesus Christ from the dead."[5] God reveals his goodwill to all of humanity. His mercy brings us to eternal life.

On the day of Jesus' crucifixion there were two other men who were led out to the hill with him, who would also be executed. They were criminals to be crucified on both sides of Jesus. These two criminals observed Jesus throughout that fateful day. They saw how he was treated badly, mocked by the soldiers and Jewish leaders. These two criminals knew their deaths were imminent. Watching Jesus, each one had a different response to him.

Luke told what he saw. Hanging beside Jesus, one of the criminals scoffed, "So you're the Messiah, are you? Prove it by saving yourself—and us, too, while you're at it!" The other criminal had a different manner and response. He replied, "Don't you even fear God when you are dying? We deserve to die for our evil deeds, but this man hasn't done one thing wrong." Then he said, "Jesus, remember me when you come into your Kingdom." Right away Jesus answered the repentant man saying, "Today you will be with me in Paradise. This is a solemn promise."[6]

That day, a dying and repentant criminal asked for mercy. With compassion, Jesus promised the man he would be with him in Paradise. The criminal with a hardened heart chose to die with his iniquities, mocking the Savior.

Jesus is a loving Savior and he offers mercy and salvation to all. When we receive the benefits of God's mercy, although unmerited, we also want others to learn of our benevolent God. For his mercies endure forever.

Peace

Peace means freedom from disturbance, a true calmness.

The writer of Psalm 119 said that the people who live by the Word have peace. "Great peace have they who love your law, and nothing can make them stumble."[7] It is the spiritual tranquility we enjoy when we have a right relationship with God. His righteousness is the basis for peace.

A friend once shared a beautiful visual for peace. Imagine a powerful roaring waterfall coming down. On the bank near the waterfall is a tree with a branch leaning over to the falls. In the branch is a nest with a dove in it. The dove is oblivious to its surroundings, peacefully resting.

One of the first Bible verses I learned as a child was a verse my mother quoted. My brother, sister, and I heard it often when we were young. She would tell us, "Blessed are the peacemakers; for they shall be called the children of God."[8]

My mother's reminder seemed to work. Most of the time, that's all it took for us siblings to try to get along with each other.

Peace does not come easily for everyone. Peace may not come easily in a world of selfishness and pride. I've observed that those who always look for trouble will find it.

But if we look for peace, we will find it. While pursuing peace we should not let bitterness destroy us or our life. In Romans Paul spoke of working hard to live peaceably with others. He told believers to "live at peace with everyone" and to "make every effort to do what leads to peace and to mutual edification."[9]

Paul also said that God's peace keeps our hearts and thoughts at rest: "And the peace of God, which transcends all understanding, will guard your hearts and your minds in Christ Jesus."[10] Peace is the fruit of the Spirit. It is the peace of God that keeps us calm. How has his peace brought calmness in your life?

It has been said, "If you want to be miserable, look within; distracted, look around; peaceful, look up."

Prayer

Lord of grace, I'm grateful for the blessings of grace, mercy, and peace. I'm thankful for your abundant grace to save and keep me. I pray for continual grace for the pressures of life and mercy for my shortcomings. Keep me from the darkness of doubt and despair with your perfect peace. Amen.

Scripture for Further Meditation

John 1:16; Romans 5:20–21; Ephesians 2:4–5; Hebrews 4:16; 2 Peter 1:2

Takeaway

When you abide in God, you will enjoy his grace, mercy, and peace.

PART FIVE
Love Him

CHAPTER 16

Long for God

"As the deer pants for streams of water,
so my soul pants for you, O God."

PSALM 42:1

It was a hot summer day. The previous months had been very dry. While I was walking on a trail by a lake, my attention turned to a doe and her fawn. The deer stood in the shallow part of the lake, lapping the cool water. The two deer glanced up every so often, paying little attention to their surroundings. Nothing would deter them from quenching their thirst, not even the noticeable movements nearby.

Instead of being in their natural surroundings, the deer were standing in the lake cooling off. Since it had not rained for months, the lush woodland surrounding the lake had become dry. Some of the vegetation had withered. I was reminded of the times when we are spiritually thirsty, desiring more of God in our lives.

In the book of Psalms, when David was living in his own thirsty land of trouble and affliction, he pleaded to God. He prayed for God to bring him relief and deliverance. He hearkened back to his days of increase, when he was satisfied.

So my spirit grows faint within me;
    my heart within me is dismayed.
I remember the days of long ago;
    I meditate on all your works
    and consider what your hands have done.

I spread out my hands to you;
>   my soul thirsts for you like a parched land.[1]

In these verses David reveals his need for God. Tasting precedes craving. David had tasted the Lord's kindness and wanted to draw close to him again.

Charles Spurgeon said, "The foundation of Christian zeal lies in the heart. . . . The heart must be vehement in desire, panting continually for God's glory, or else we shall never attain to anything like the zeal, which God would have us know."[2]

The prophet Hosea exhorted God's people to be wholeheartedly devoted to God. He explained they must turn their focus to spiritual and eternal things, gaining spiritual knowledge. He addressed the Israelites saying, "There is no faithfulness, no love, no acknowledgment of God in the land."[3] Israel needed to repent, return to the Lord, and restore the relationship.

Hosea spoke of the immense and tender love God had for Israel. He also spoke of how the people deserted the worship of God and instead mixed religions freely and worshiped idols. They rejected God's wisdom and his ways, allowing their relationship with him to be broken. God was deeply disappointed in them. Nevertheless, he continued to persevere for their reciprocal love.

Hosea said:

Let us acknowledge the LORD;
>   let us press on to acknowledge him.
"As surely as the sun rises,
>   he will appear;
he will come to us like the winter rains,
>   like the spring rains that water the earth."[4]

Living a victorious life includes continually seeking more of God and his will for us. Wanting to live in the center of his will, we seek to discover the truths he has for our lives.

Most Christians can recall times when they had mountain-top experiences. These are rich encounters with God that moved us, stirring us to action.

When I was six years old I had my first mountain-top experience. In my room at boarding school my roommate and I had been talking about spiritual things. It dawned on me that I didn't know if I was a child of God. I realized that not only did Jesus die for everyone but that he died for me, for my own sins.

Then the topic turned to where I would spend eternity. I knew that I tried to be good and obedient. I also knew I was a sinner. I knew my parents talked about the importance of loving Jesus. But he didn't seem real to me. And I guess I didn't know for sure where my home would be when I died.

God moved upon my heart, and I knew I needed to make an important decision. That evening I knelt by the bunk bed beside my roommate. I accepted Christ as my Lord and Savior. I recall the joy I felt after praying to receive him into my life. I felt free and I knew I had a Friend for life.

As a teenager, one evening at a youth camp I had another mountain-top experience. A missionary had just spoken to a large crowd of teens. He spoke of the importance of dedicating our lives to God, for this was an important time of life for us. We would make many essential decisions in the coming years ahead.

After the close of the service, as I left the tent and found a moment by myself, I felt God's presence and sensed that I needed to dedicate my life to him. With no hesitation I did, wanting to be obedient to him.

Under the starry skies that night, I talked to God. I asked him to direct my life in my formative years and beyond. His presence was real and I was overjoyed. It was hard for me to go to sleep that night, for I couldn't wait to see what God had in store for me.

Can you think back to mountain-top experiences you've had with God? How did they change you?

Our deep love for our heavenly Father leads us to want to know more of him and his ways. We do this by hearing and reading the Bible, for God speaks to us through his Word and by his Holy Spirit. With a receptive heart and mind, we learn of him.

Having been cleansed from our old ways, we obey him. We "have purified [ourselves] by obeying the truth."[5] Obedience leads to a life of God's blessings in our lives.

Jesus said, "If you obey my commands, you will remain in my love."[6] Obedience shows God and others the reality of Christ in our lives. Genuine faith shows itself through spiritual action.

Love and faith work together wonderfully in our lives. Love and faith mature together. The more we show our love for Christ, the more our faith in him is evident.

In the same way that deer long for cool water, may we continue to yearn for a close relationship with our Creator. He is the object of our innermost longing.

When wandering into the dry times of our life, may we turn to the right path of renewal. David called out to God, "My soul thirsts for God, for the living God."[7] When was the last time you felt you were living in your own thirsty land? What helped you best when facing times of spiritual dryness?

May our lives continue to receive sustenance from him. He has infinite love for us, and it is he who sustains us. We thank him for his loving-kindness. We pray that our zeal for him will never end.

Prayer
Lord, I praise you for your loving-kindness that continues forever. When I wander into the dry times of my life, turn me onto the right path to renewal. I am longing for more of you and pray my zeal for you will never end. Amen.

Scripture for Further Meditation
Psalm 42:4–8; Psalm 77:11–15; Psalm 107:8–9; Isaiah 26:9

Takeaway
When you love God, you will want to know and experience more of him and his ways.

CHAPTER 17

Guard Your Heart

"Above all else, guard your heart, for it is the wellspring of life."

PROVERBS 4:23

When I was a young girl, our family lived in a rain forest region of Brazil. After a typical heavy rainfall, the rainwater would steadily flow throughout the rain forest, creating natural streams and pools.

Sometimes our family would go to a natural stream near our home. At one particular spot the rainwater cascaded off a steep slope, collecting in a deep pond below. I recall playing and swimming in the newly formed pond. It was refreshing to bask in the crystal clear waters. The natural stream flowed forth from its source of water—fresh rain falling from the sky above. This special pool was a place of tranquility.

Just as the rainwater leads to a flowing stream, our heart is the wellspring of life. King Solomon is known for his great wisdom. He said, "Watch over your heart with all diligence, for from it flow the springs of life."[1] This is a father's instruction that wisdom is supreme. The way of wisdom is a less traveled path. But it is a straight path that will not cause us to stumble. Those who walk it do so securely. Esteem wisdom and have a good and long life.

How can we walk in wisdom and prosper from it? We must guard our heart.

Andrew Murray, revered writer and minister of his day, wrote on matters of the heart. He challenged believers to be examples of uncompromising holiness. He said, "With the heart, man believes and comes into touch with God. In the heart, God has given his Spirit. It is the heart that must trust, love, worship, and obey. My mind is utterly inadequate in creating or maintaining the spiritual life within me. The heart must wait on God for him to work it in me."[2]

Our heart is the fountain of our life, the very essence of our nature. What comes from our inner being flows out, revealing who we are. What we believe, think, or feel is the source of how we live our lives.

If we desire to live a life for God, it will not come about without guarding our heart. We must stand vigilant to set our affections on what pleases God. Despite having a new life with the new nature, we still live in an ungodly world system.

David loved God and wanted to please him. Yet, in weak moments, he gave in to temptation. What followed were tragic consequences for him. Later David acknowledged his transgressions to God. Remorseful, he prayed, "Create in me a pure heart, O God, and renew a steadfast spirit within me."[3] Although sorry for his deeds, David acknowledged that his sins continued to affect him and the ones he loved adversely.

God removes the filth from our unclean heart when he forgives our sins. He gives us a pure heart. Jesus said, "Blessed are the pure in heart, for they will see God."[4] It is up to us to diligently keep the wellspring of our life clean and undefiled. He will help keep us from sin and from the effects of sin.

Our highest priority must be to watch over and guard our heart. Jesus said, "The good man brings good things out of the good stored in his heart, and the evil man brings evil things out of the evil stored up in his heart. For out of the overflow of his heart his mouth speaks."[5] To guard our heart effectively we must stand strong and resist wrong influences.

Protect your heart from the distractions of the world that invade our culture. Be continually sensitive to the nudgings of the Holy Spirit, watching the intentions of your heart. Depending on God to empower you, live a clean and god-fearing life. For we are accountable to him. What are some ways you can guard your heart more diligently?

Frequently we must ask ourselves, "Who is in control of my life?" Sometimes things do not always go right when we are in control. Examining our motivations and actions, we may need to confess our sins and failings and ask for God's forgiveness. Let him be in control again. Thank him for all the good things that will come.

As we go on to maturity and master our inner being, our heart will overflow with good things, pleasing to our Lord.

One ship goes east, another west,
By the same winds they blow;
It's the set of the sail and not the gale,
That determines the way they go.
Like the winds of the sea are the ways of time,
As we voyage along through life;
It's the set of the soul that determines the goal,
And not the calm or the strife.[6]

Prayer
Lord and Savior, as King David prayed, Create in me a new heart.
Nudge me often to examine my heart and keep watch over it.
I desire to stand vigilant and on guard. Amen.

Scripture for Further Meditation
1 Samuel 16:7; Psalm 51:10–12; Psalm 119:26; Jeremiah 17:9;
Matthew 5:8

Takeaway
When you love God, you will keep your heart clean
with all diligence.

CHAPTER 18

Worship God

"Ascribe to the Lord the glory due his name;
worship the Lord in the splendor of his holiness."

PSALM 29:2

In worship we give wholehearted attention to God, considering and dwelling upon the beauty of his holiness. We declare his greatness and goodness to us. He is worthy to be praised. The Eternal One is adored.

To worship is to know and experience the presence of God. The glory—the radiance of God's holiness—actively dwells in the midst of his people. The glory of God is a culture of heaven. It is three entities working together. They are God the Father, God the Son, and God the Holy Spirit.

Worship makes an important contribution to our spiritual growth. As believers, we engage in this important discipline. It is our response to our heavenly Father's abundant love touching us. We respond naturally to his divine initiative. There is an encounter between the Creator and his creation. Worship is kindled in us as his Holy Spirit touches our spirit, drawing us closer to him. God gives us reason and speech that help us appreciate him and make known our devotion to him.

God is looking for worshipers. Jesus said, "True worshipers will worship the Father in spirit and truth, for they are the kind of worshipers the Father seeks. God is spirit, and his worshipers must worship in spirit and in truth."[1] True worship springs forth from the inside. It is genuine and sincere.

As we take part in authentic worship we open our hearts and our lives to the Holy One. We are allowed to experience the heavenly realm . . . God's presence, his glory, and his holiness. At ease, we experience real peace.

We worship the Lord as a way of expressing our love for him. When there is absence of worship, there is something missing in the relationship. When there is absence of praise, there is probably an inadequate view of a holy God.

When God is truly the Lord of our lives, worship is an important part of our lives. In fact, we make it a priority.

We worship God for who he is. We are amazed at the revelation of his nature in Jesus Christ. Consider his infinite knowledge and wisdom. There is no end to his love and mercy. God is exalted and we acknowledge his greatness.

Ponder on his attributes. God is . . .

✧ Triune—Three "persons" unified into one God
✧ Holy—Righteous and pure
✧ Infinite —Unlimited and unlimitable
✧ Eternal—Free from the succession of time
✧ Sovereign—Supreme ruler
✧ Omnipresent—Everywhere at all times
✧ Omniscient—Knowing all actual and possible things
✧ Omnipotent—All-powerful
✧ Just—Morally equitable
✧ Love—Seeking the highest good

We also worship God for what he has done. The psalmist wrote, "Let them give thanks to the Lord for his unfailing love and his wonderful deeds for men, for he satisfies the thirsty and fills the hungry with good things."[2]

The Giver of every good gift is exalted. Think about his goodness to us. It is impossible to exaggerate his goodness. Not only are his kind acts made known throughout history, but they also continue in our own lives.

The Father receives our adoration, praise, and thanksgiving. The writer of Hebrews advised us, "Let us continually offer to God a sacrifice of praise—the fruit of lips that confess his name."[3] We declare his wonderful deeds made plain to us. "For since the creation of the world God's invisible qualities—his eternal power and divine nature—have been clearly seen, being understood from what has been made, so that men are without excuse."[4]

When we worship God, we can worship him when we are alone. In solitude, we can have times of praise and adoration.

We can also worship regularly with other believers. It's good to assemble with one another. Being part of a church family brings about fellowship with others. These friendships unite us, allowing us to encourage each other. They help move us forward in the Christian life. Attending a local church brings opportunities for spiritual growth.

As a young girl my parents taught us children the importance of worshiping God on Sunday. It was a natural thing for us to do. This is a day set aside to honor the Lord. When our family was traveling, Dad would find a church we could attend. When there wasn't a local church around, our family would have a familial time of worship to God. We'd meet together on the beach, in a cabin, or wherever our travels took us.

Reading Scripture, praying, and singing move us into praise. God reveals himself to us as we read and study his Word. Knowing and understanding his revelation leads us to respond in worship.

In our prayers we experience the presence of God, expressing our praise and thanksgiving. Giving thanks is an act of praise inspired by God's faithfulness. We are to "pray continually."[5]

In our singing we give praise to God. Through songs we express our thanks and joy for who God is and what he has done. Throughout Scriptures we are reminded to sing unto the Lord.

The book of Psalms provides us with many psalms of praise and thanksgiving. In the Hebrew language it is known as the book of Praises, from the Hebrew word meaning *joyful sounds* or *praises*. In Greek, the word for psalms means *songs*. The Psalms have been used in worship since the time of David. It is often called the Prayer Book of the Bible.

Psalm 100 is a well-known psalm for giving thanks.

Shout for joy to the Lord, all the earth.
   Worship the Lord with gladness;
   come before him with joyful songs.
Know that the Lord is God.
   It is he who made us, and we are his;
   we are his people, the sheep of his pasture.

Enter his gates with thanksgiving
   and his courts with praise;
   give thanks to him and praise his name.
For the Lord is good and his love endures forever;
   his faithfulness continues through all generations.

Some of us may have been in a dry place spiritually for quite a long time. Or perhaps there are shorter durations where our spiritual life seems parched and lackluster. Just as the sun is hidden from us on a cloudy, overcast day, we may feel God is hidden from us. Perhaps it seems he is unreachable. Yet he loves to dwell among his people.

When we do not sense God's nearness, there is something we can do to receive his presence. Jesus' teachings indicate that the Father seeks people who will worship him. When we praise and worship him he comes to receive his praises, for God inhabits the praises of his people.

For the ones who have been missing the closeness and presence of God, perhaps worship is the missing ingredient. Are you setting aside time each week to worship God? When you worship God do you give wholehearted attention to him with adoration, praise, and thanksgiving?

When we praise God, it will seem as though the sun is breaking out through the gray and overcast sky. Assuredly, our days will brighten and our heart will rejoice.

Prayer

Awesome God, thank you that through worship you reveal yourself to me. I praise you, rejoicing in your goodness and greatness. Your glory is declared among the nations. May my love for you be evident as I worship you. Amen.

Scripture for Further Meditation

Psalm 105:1–4; Ephesians 5:19–20; Hebrews 13:15; Revelation 4:11

Takeaway

When you love God, you will want to worship him.

CHAPTER 19

Pursue Holiness

"Let us purify ourselves . . .
perfecting holiness out of reverence for God."

2 CORINTHIANS 7:1

A. B. Simpson said, "It is not the world that stains us, but the love of the world."[1]

In our culture we are besieged with the world's immoral ways all around us. Our children, young people, and families are not immune to its ways. Yet God continues to draw us to a life of holiness. We know as believers we are *in* the world and not *of* the world.

In the church there has been a lack of teaching on the topic of holy living. Holiness is purity in thought, word, and action. It is the nature and character of God in a person. Since God dwells in us, we set ourselves completely apart for God to use us. We are made new in Christ, created to be holy. We have his nature and character. He is working in us, perfecting us.

What do you think "perfecting holiness" means, as stated in the key verse of 2 Corinthians 7:1?

We know holy living begins with a healthy respect for the Lord. We give him our honor, obedience, and reverence. There is an ongoing desire to follow and obey him. As we grow in our love for God, we grow in our relationship with him. We love what he loves and hate what he hates.

God wants his people to be free from dirt or stain when we come to him and worship him. In the Old Testament, a way to achieve ceremonial cleansing was by water. The tabernacle courtyards had lavers, or basins, for the washing of hands and feet. The priests and Levites stopped regularly to wash at the lavers that stood between the tent and the altar. The Levites continually replenished the lavers with clean water.

Water for washing is represented by the Word of God. When we are made unclean by sin, it is the "washing with water through the word" that cleanses us.[2] The Word sanctifies us. It cleanses our hearts and minds when we accept and obey it. Our ways are kept pure when we live according to the Word.

If we have not been cleansed we cannot enjoy fellowship with God. Turning from sinful ways restores this fellowship. David said, "Create in me a pure heart, O God, and renew a steadfast spirit within me. Do not cast me from your presence or take your Holy Spirit from me. Restore to me the joy of your salvation and grant me a willing spirit, to sustain me."[3]

Paul explained that believers are dead to sin. Having been freed from sin we now belong to God. Our benefit is a life of holiness and eternal life with him.[4] When we are in a right relationship with God, holy living is our spiritual fruit.

Do we *know* God or do we know *about* God? Some believers have a lot of knowledge of God in their head, yet they want something more from him in their lives. It is important to root out unrighteous ways and perfect godly character.

God may bring things to our mind that we need to deal with, one at a time. Perhaps something is keeping us from moving forward in victory. An unconfessed sin or failure may be weighing us down, as a boat tied down by a heavy anchor. Or it could be something in our way of life that holds us back. It is holding us back from making spiritual progress.

We may feel unworthy and hesitant to approach the Father with our needs and concerns. Our guilt and feelings of unworthiness can get between us. But God is accessible. It is up to us to come boldly before him.

The prophet Jeremiah spoke about the deceitful heart. He said, "The heart is deceitful above all things and beyond cure. Who can understand it? I the LORD search the heart and examine the mind, to reward a man according to his conduct, according to what his deeds deserve."[5] All of us have this heart condition. However, there is a Helper, for the Holy Spirit lives in us. He convicts and lovingly shows us the truth.

Jesus has delivered us from the power of sin. "For the grace of God that brings salvation has appeared to all men. It teaches us to say 'No' to ungodliness and worldly passions, and to live self-controlled, upright and godly lives in this present age."[6] When we discern, we perceive and judge wisely. We are able to see things from God's perspective.

In his letter to the believers in Philippi, Paul encouraged them to be able to discern what was excellent and to be "pure and blameless"[7] until the end. He said, "For God is at work within you, helping you want to obey him, and then helping you do what he wants."[8]

Sometimes when we have hardships there is a sense we are being purified. These experiences cause times of introspection. Perhaps the Holy Spirit is giving us new insights into his ways. During these times, be sure to pray for an open and receptive heart.

Paul taught the believers to guard their hearts and minds. He told them to think on the things that are true, noble, right, pure, lovely and admirable. Think on things that are excellent or praiseworthy.[9]

The psalmist David talked about the importance of living a holy life. He said, "Who may ascend the hill of the LORD? Who may stand in his holy place? He who has clean hands and a pure heart, who does not lift up his soul to an idol or swear by what is false. He will receive blessing from the LORD."[10]

We probably agree that we can't get cleansed in dirty water. If we want clean hands, we need clean water. If we want a pure heart, we need to seek a life of purity.

A few years ago my husband went on a short-term missions trip to Peru. He went with a group to help share the gospel with the people in the villages. He learned during that visit that even though clean water is offered to people, many of them continue to use dirty water.

New ground wells were dug on earlier trips. Each well was equipped with a hand pump to prime the water. Surely the villagers would benefit greatly from this water. If they drank this clean water and washed in it, they wouldn't need to worry about getting sick so often. The children wouldn't die at an early age. The adults would live longer.

But instead of drinking the clean water from the well and washing in the water, the people continued to use the dirty river water near their village. Some of them said they didn't like the taste of the well water. They were content to keep their old ways of doing things, even though the river water caused diseases and illnesses. Though it shortened their life spans, many of them would continue to use the dirty water.

I am reminded that today some people are using the world's ways to try to get spiritually clean. Their attempts do not erase the filth. The world's ways affect the quality of their lives and their health negatively. They are stuck in a cycle only they can break.

The cycle can be broken, however. Whoever wants to can have clean hands and a pure heart. He or she can reach out to a holy God. Is there anything holding you back from living a life pleasing to God?

We can go boldly to the throne of grace and receive the help we need. The prayers of the saints rise before the Lord. And Jesus intercedes for us. He is our advocate and our defender. John said, "If our hearts do not condemn us, we have confidence before God and receive from him anything we ask, because we obey his commands and do what pleases him."[11] The original Greek word for "confidence" means *boldness*, or *the freedom to speak boldly*. It is because of who we are in Jesus Christ that we can speak boldly to God.

Having a genuine faith will cause us to get rid of any known sin and things that pollute our lives. We can humbly accept the word that saves and delivers us. Then we can continue to put the Scriptures into practice. When we seek God's help, allowing him to work in our lives, the result is right living. He continues to restore our lives and to bring fullness of joy.

Prayer

Righteous Lord, you are worthy to receive my praises. I magnify your name. Protect me from the distractions of the world that invade our culture. Guide me to do what pleases you. Amen.

Scripture for Further Meditation

Psalm 19:9; Romans 2:13–16; Romans 6:22; Philippians 4:8; Hebrews 10:22

Takeaway

When you love God and respect him, he releases his power in your life in greater measure. This enables proper living.

PART SIX
Walk with Him

CHAPTER 20

God Is Our Hope

"Those who hope in the LORD will renew their strength.
They will soar on wings like eagles; they will run and not grow weary,
they will walk and not be faint."

ISAIAH 40:31

Hope is an essential characteristic of the Christian. It is linked with faith. This is a quality that encompasses an ultimate confidence and trust in God. It connotes safety and refuge in him.

The eagle has long been a sign of strength and freedom. It is one of the largest birds in the world. A majestic bird, it is known for its swiftness, gracefulness, and elegance.

Since I live in a region where the bald eagle makes its home, I am able to observe this bird closely. It has pure white plumage on its head, neck, and tail, and dark brown feathers on most of its body. The eagle's beak, legs, and feet are very strong. Its keen vision gives it a distinct advantage.

Many times I have seen eagles gracefully encircling their nest before perching there. The eagle, with a wide wingspread, soars beautifully in the sky. Surprisingly, the bird's long wing feathers are quite firm. The eagle can glide easily in an updraft, with the air currents flowing above the wings' surface. The eagle flies swiftly and confidently, often gliding long distances.

The strength of the eagle is often compared to the fortitude and endurance granted to people who hope in the Lord. God continues to sustain us, giving renewed determination and confidence.

We can be certain that he watches over us. As an eagle spreads its wings over its young to protect them, God takes care of the righteous.

We read in Isaiah that it is the Lord God who is our source of strength.

Do you not know?
Have you not heard?
The Lord is the everlasting God,
the Creator of the ends of the earth.
He will not grow tired or weary,
and his understanding no one can fathom.
He gives strength to the weary
and increases the power of the weak.[1]

When God spoke to Moses in the Desert of Sinai, he spoke of eagles' wings. He said, "You yourselves have seen what I did to Egypt, and how I carried you on eagles' wings and brought you to myself."[2]

David spoke of the eagle when he praised God for all his glorious works. He said it is God "who satisfies your desires with good things so that your youth is renewed like the eagle's."[3] We can count on him to renew us, filling our lives with good things.

The words in Psalm 33 tell us to put our trust in the God of hope. Scripture says,

We wait in hope for the Lord;
he is our help and our shield.
In him our hearts rejoice,
for we trust in his holy name.
May your unfailing love rest upon us, O Lord,
even as we put our hope in you.[4]

At times we may feel as though we are drowning in a sea of doubt and despair. We may be saddened by difficulties in life. Yet our hope is in the Lord. He gives us purpose and meaning in life. As we trust him, he gives us hope. We find safety through the storms of life. Scriptures assure us that our hope is secure in Christ. In Hebrews this hope is compared to a firm and secure anchor for the soul.[5]

When we hope in the Lord, we wait on him. But since waiting is not easy, it is natural to want to resist waiting. We find that, in the Christian walk, we often want results right away. There may not be quick answers or easy answers.

But we can decide to pray about our concerns and wait upon our heavenly Father for the answers. He promised to meet our needs. Moreover, we have an Advocate before the throne of grace.

We have trusted in God for our salvation. Surely we can trust him for the difficult situations that arise in life. When we ponder on the character of our heavenly Father, it is reasonable to rejoice in the God of hope.

How has placing your hope in God made a difference in your life?

When we place our hope and trust in the Omnipotent One, we find new strength. We come to him with expectation and confidence. He gives endurance, helping us soar high above life's difficult challenges.

Prayer
Sovereign God, with my trust and confidence in you,
I come to you. When I am discouraged and weary, renew me
with your strength. Help me to keep my eyes on you.
My hope is in you. Amen.

Scripture for Further Meditation
Psalm 42:5–6; Romans 15:4; Ephesians 1:18–19; 1 Timothy 6:17;
Titus 2:13; Hebrews 10:23

Takeaway
When you walk with God, you can look forward with confidence
to receive the good things God has promised.

CHAPTER 21

He Is the Good Shepherd

"I am the good shepherd;
I know my sheep and my sheep know me."

JOHN 10:14

When I was a child I looked forward to visiting friends who lived on a large farm. There were many sheep on the farm. I watched them graze and frolic in the green hilly pastures. Some of the sheep seemed unafraid to meander from the flock. On sunny afternoons they appeared to be especially content.

One day I observed the farmer rounding up his sheep. He gathered them to shear their overgrown and scraggly wool. As he reached down to nab the sheep, some leaped to get away. They stumbled away in different directions. Others yielded willingly. Once the sheep were in the hands of the one whose voice they knew, one by one they were sheared skillfully and then released.

We read in the Old Testament that David was a shepherd boy before becoming Israel's king. Abel, Abraham, and Rachel also kept flocks of sheep. They led the sheep to water and good grazing land. Knowing the sheep were likely to go astray, these shepherds watched over them carefully. Guiding them, the shepherds helped the sheep find their way.

Sheep are inherently weak. When attacked, they are naturally helpless. They will huddle together and cry, bleating for help. Sheep depend on their faithful shepherd to protect them. They love their shepherd for he shows his tender care to them.

In Isaiah, we are compared to sheep that have gone astray. Each of us has gone his or her own way.[1] Like a good shepherd, God cares for his flock. He gathers the lambs and carries them near to his heart. He leads the sheep with lambs.[2]

We read in the New Testament that Jesus had compassion on the crowds "because they were harassed and helpless, like sheep without a shepherd.[3] He did not look on the people with condemnation but with love.

One day Jesus told the parable of the lost sheep. He speculated, suppose someone has one hundred sheep and one leaves the fold. Will he not search for the lost sheep until it is found? Upon locating the lone sheep he will carry him home. Then with joy he will get his neighbors and friends together, telling them to be happy with him. His sheep was found! Jesus said, "In the same way there will be more rejoicing in heaven over one sinner who repents than over ninety-nine righteous persons who do not need to repent."[4]

When speaking to the people, Jesus described himself as the good shepherd. He explained that the good shepherd is one who lays down his life for the sheep.[5] He knows the sheep and they know and follow him. His sheep listen to his voice. They will never perish, since he has come so they will have life. The enemy wants to devour the sheep from his flock. But no one can take them away from the shepherd's hand.

Jesus also said he is the gate for the sheep. During Bible times some shepherds tending their sheep in the countryside built a sheepfold or walled enclosure, usually of rough stone. The enclosure was covered with thorns intended to keep thieves away. The shepherd stayed at the narrow sheepfold entrance, protecting the sheep in the fold. Jesus said, "I am the gate; whoever enters through me will be saved. . . . The thief comes only to steal and kill and destroy; I have come that they may have life, and have it to the full."[6]

Jesus is the doorway to salvation. All of us must decide whether we will enter through the narrow way. Jesus has come to give us life in all its fullness. The good news is that the gift of life includes eternal life in heaven with him. For Jesus stated, "I give them eternal life, and they shall never perish; no one can snatch them out of my hand."[7]

Peter reminded the new believers of their changed way of life. He said they had previously gone astray as sheep. But now they had returned to their Shepherd. They returned to the Overseer of their souls[8] and would be rewarded someday. He also said when believers are in heaven we "will share in the glory to be revealed."[9] Our gracious God has invited us to share in his wonderful eternal glory.

We have heard the voice of our Shepherd and follow him. He protects and directs us. How well do we follow him?

Wanting to please our Master and Lord, we will stay close to him. He is trustworthy and faithful, leading us to green pastures of hope and love and joy.

Prayer
Loving God, thank you for being the Good Shepherd of your people. You guide and protect me, keeping me in your care. Continue to lead me until I dwell forever with you in heaven. Amen.

Scripture for Further Meditation
Psalm 23:1–6; Psalm 95:6–7; Psalm 100:3; John 10:1-4

Takeaway
When you walk with the Good Shepherd, he will lead you and take care of you.

CHAPTER 22

Walk in His Presence

"You have made known to me the path of life;
you will fill me with joy in your presence,
with eternal pleasures at your right hand."

PSALM 16:11

One of the paintings in our home has special value to me. In the past, my parents displayed the painting in their home. It is *The Road to Emmaus*, showing a depiction of Jesus walking with two of his followers after his resurrection. This idyllic painting reminds me of our walk with the Lord.

The artist is Robert Zund, an important Swiss painter of the nineteenth century. Having lived in the countryside near Lucerne, he developed a special affinity to nature. He enjoyed painting scenic landscapes with elaborate detail. The Swiss Protestant's faith is displayed through the many biblical motifs in his works of art.

Depicting a scene from Luke 24, *The Road to Emmaus* shows the disciples' captive attention as they listen to the Teacher. In the countryside and surrounded by tall oak trees, they are walking on a narrow dirt path. It is a peaceful and calm scene.

Luke was a convert and disciple in the early church. He recorded on paper eyewitness accounts of what happened in the life of Jesus. In this beautiful account he told about an actual encounter of two traveling companions and Jesus. I will retell the story.

After his resurrection, Jesus appeared to two of his disciples as they were walking from Jerusalem to their small village of Emmaus.

The journey was a distance of about seven miles. Cleopas and his fellow disciple were returning home after observing the Passover and the Feast of the Unleavened Bread. Heartbroken and discouraged, they were discussing what had happened in Jerusalem. Their dreams of Jesus taking over as the new ruler of the land had turned into the reality of his death at Calvary. They believed Jesus was the One who would set Israel free from Roman occupation, redeeming them from their oppressive situation. But Jesus was crucified. *Why did he have to die?* his disciples wondered.

As they talked about the events, Christ approached them and asked what they were discussing. Not recognizing the stranger, they asked, "With so much happening in Jerusalem lately, how could it be you haven't heard about it yet?"

"Tell me about these things," he answered. He walked with them and listened.

The disciples talked about Jesus of Nazareth, whom they believed was a powerful and mighty prophet. They knew of his miracles. They expected him to be the Redeemer of Israel, for they believed he was the Messiah. But then Jesus was nailed to the cross. His crucifixion erased their hopes for a new king. But there is more. . . . That day they even heard reports from the women that the tomb was empty and Jesus was alive, but they did not believe them.

Rather than believing the news he was alive, they were astonished and confused. Things seemed to make little sense to them.

Having listened to their animated conversation, Jesus rebuked them for their unbelief.

Jesus said, "How could you be without understanding and not perceive all the things the prophets have spoken?" If they had not been so dull, they would have known and believed that Christ would need to suffer death and then enter his glory. The disciples' real problem was what was in their hearts. They did not believe everything the prophets wrote concerning the Messiah.

Then Jesus guided the conversation, reminding them that what had happened in Jerusalem was morally necessary. The greatest Teacher explained to them what was said in the Scriptures about himself. Beginning with Moses and all the Prophets, Jesus opened the Scriptures to them in a new way. He explained to them that Jesus was the conquering Redeemer and King, and he was the Suffering Servant. He explained how the crown and the suffering went together. The King of the Jews had become a sin offering, a most holy offering.

As the disciples walked and listened to Jesus, they became encouraged. The truths of his Word and his presence encouraged them.

When the men approached Emmaus they invited the Teacher to stay with them, since it was later in the day. After the illuminating discussion Jesus had with them, they wanted to spend more time with this amazing person. He had opened the Scriptures to them in a way that touched their lives. They wanted to fellowship with him and continue in his presence.

At their invitation Jesus stayed with them and joined them for the evening meal. Sitting with them at the table, he took the unleavened bread and thanked God for it and broke it, as a host of the home would do. As he started to give the bread to the men, they fully recognized him. Then in an instant Jesus disappeared from their sight.

When Jesus was breaking the bread, his followers saw his pierced hands and knew. Their eyes were opened, and they had a new understanding about their guest. They had been with the risen Christ! He was no longer dead. They were astonished. "They asked each other, 'Were not our hearts burning within us while he talked with us on the road and opened the Scriptures to us?'"[1] There was something about his presence that encouraged them and drew them to him.

With renewed hope and joy, the disciples knew that although Jesus had disappeared from their sight, he had not abandoned them. Energized by what had just happened, right away they returned to Jerusalem, meeting with the eleven apostles and others. They could not stop talking about what had happened.

Cleopas and his friend told the apostles it was true that the Lord had risen! Then they told the group about their actual encounter with Jesus. They reported what happened earlier that day as they walked home to Emmaus. They had seen Jesus and walked with him. His presence warmed their hearts. They explained how they recognized Jesus when he broke bread with them.

Do you feel close to God? Do you need to get rid of any doubt in your life?

God will make himself known to us as we seek him and seek to know more of him. He will fill us with joy as we walk in his presence, as did Jesus' two companions on resurrection day. He changes us with his life-changing power.

Perhaps we need to get rid of things that hinder our walk with the Lord. Let us not take a wrong path that distracts us from God. Let us walk in the right paths.

When we experience disappointment and hard times, we should remember that God continues to accompany us on our Christian walk. We were designed for closeness with him. He is with us.

Prayer
Almighty God, thank you for walking with me.
You bring strength for the journey. Your presence sustains
me and you are forever faithful. Amen.

Scripture for Further Meditation
Psalm 119:1–3; Proverbs 10:9–10; John 14:16–18; John 16:13

Takeaway
When you walk with God, you will enjoy his presence.
He'll be with you always.

CHAPTER 23

Be a Light in the World

"You are the light of the world.
A city on a hill cannot be hidden."
MATTHEW 5:14

The worship service was almost over. Our pastor invited everyone in the congregation to participate in the lighting of candles. The electric lighting in the sanctuary was dimmed. Starting at the front of the church, each candle was lit. Slowly, the candlelight spread from the front and the middle of the sanctuary to the back rows.

It was no longer dark. The candlelight shined for all, radiant and bright. Singing the final songs of worship and holding the lit candles, we were reminded that in this world we are to be the light bearers. We are to carry the light in the world and to the world.

Jesus is the light of the world. Whoever chooses to follow the light will not walk in darkness. Instead, he will have the light of life.[1] When did God rescue you out of the darkness into his wonderful light?

Believers have received spiritual life, having received the knowledge of God. Jesus, our spiritual light, also provides us with the highest kind of life, eternal life.

Since God is merciful he sent his Son to a dark and dying world. Christ has come "to shine on those living in darkness and in the shadow of death, to guide our feet into the path of peace."[2] Jesus Christ shines light upon those who live in darkness, showing himself openly before the people. He has come for those in sin and misery.

When Jesus was a baby, his parents took him to the temple at Jerusalem. They went to consecrate him to the Lord and to offer a sacrifice. At that time, it was revealed by the Holy Spirit to Simeon, a righteous and devout man in Jerusalem, that he should go to the temple courts. When he got there he saw a special baby.

Holding baby Jesus in his arms, he praised God. Simeon said, "For my eyes have seen your salvation, which you have prepared in the sight of all people, a light for revelation to the Gentiles and for glory to your people Israel."[3] Delighted to meet the baby, Simeon knew this little One was the light to all people and the Savior of the world.

People are either living in darkness or light. Jesus came to overcome moral darkness and spiritual darkness.

People that do evil hate the light. People reject the light and they do not want their sinful condition and deeds exposed. They refuse to accept God's glorious gift of the pure light, Jesus Christ. Persons in darkness prefer their sinful lives over the pure light of the Righteous One. Unless they look for the light in Jesus Christ, they will not see it.

God has reconciled us through his Son. The apostle Paul said, "Once you were alienated from God and were enemies in your minds because of your evil behavior. But now he has reconciled you."[4] Now that we belong to God we thank him that he called us "out of darkness into his wonderful light."[5]

When Jesus was dying on the cross, during the last three hours there was darkness all over the land. At the moment Jesus died at Calvary, the thick curtain in the temple of Jerusalem was ripped in half from top to bottom. It had sealed off the Most Holy Place, allowing only the high priest to have access to the presence of God in the temple.

Suddenly the curtain in the temple was torn. There was instant access to God through Jesus, the mediator for all. Just as the veil in the temple was gone, so God also removes the veil of blindness from people's eyes and hearts.

But there are still people blinded to the gospel. Paul said, "The god of this age has blinded the minds of unbelievers, so that they cannot see the light of the gospel of the glory of Christ, who is the image of God."[6] It is through the power of God that the lost come to know the living Savior. Remember to pray for unbelievers that they would see the glorious light of the gospel.

We are the light of the world. We as believers have been called out of darkness and God is using us as light bearers. Jesus said, "I am sending you to them to open their eyes and turn them from darkness to light."[7]

Christ's light shines on us and he says, "Arise, shine." Since Christians are lights in the world, how strong would you say your light shines? Is it dim or steadily giving off light?

We are to reflect the radiant light of Christ. May we shine our light before others that they may see our good works, and glorify our heavenly Father.[8]

The Christian life is compared to a walk. It starts with a step of faith and leads to a walk of faith. We have no love for sin, but continue to have real fellowship with him. A way to have a close relationship with him is to know his Word. God's Word to us is truth. King David said, "Your word is a lamp to my feet and a light for my path."[9]

Years ago when I was a child our family lived in an undeveloped part of Brazil. For a few hours in the evening we had electricity powered by a generator.

When we didn't have electric power we relied on our kerosene lamps. At night when all was dark around me, I held my lamp before me. It showed the path for me to go, lighting the way. I needed just enough light to see the path ahead of me.

When we walk in the light, we are made brighter as lights in the world. When we compromise with the world's ways, our lights are dim. John wrote: "If we claim to have fellowship with [God] yet walk in the darkness, we lie and do not live by the truth. But if we walk in the light, as he is in the light, we have fellowship with one another, and the blood of Jesus, his Son, purifies us from all sin."[10]

Believers who walk in the light not only enjoy fellowship with God, they also enjoy fellowship with other Christians. I realized this truth as a young adult.

I attended graduate school at a state university. In one particular class, a counseling class, we had frequent group discussions. We moved our chairs to form a large circle and talked about topics our professor assigned to us. He asked us to be willing to share openly in his large class.

After class one day a young lady came up to me. She asked, "Are you a Christian?"

Without hesitation I told her, "Yes, I am."

With a smile she said, "I thought you were. I'm a pastor's wife and it's sure nice to have another Christian in our class!"

That evening I learned that others in class had been watching me. And apparently I was being a light in my class.

God has shown us a lighted and secure path for our lives. Paul said, "Live as children of light (for the fruit of the light consists in all goodness, righteousness and truth) and find out what pleases the Lord."[11]

As you walk through life, are you walking the way that is lighted and straight? Walking in the light simply means you are living to please God and obeying him.

Prayer

Lord of the Word, I'm thankful you brought the light of the gospel into this dark and sinful world. Help my light to shine brightly. I pray for my family members and friends, knowing you want to turn them from darkness to light, opening their eyes to the truth of your Word. Thank you for drawing them to yourself. Amen.

Scripture for Further Meditation

Psalm 119:129–130; Philippians 1:27; 1 Thessalonians 2:12; 1 John 1:1–9

Takeaway

When you walk with God in the light, he shows you the right paths to take.

PART SEVEN
Live for Him

CHAPTER 24

It's About Time

"Teach us to number our days aright,
that we may gain a heart of wisdom."

PSALM 90:12

With each day that passes, are you gaining a heart of wisdom? We do not gain wisdom passively. It comes by reverence for God. We grow in wisdom by accepting his words and living closely with him. True wisdom is the ability to take knowledge and make good decisions. It encompasses knowledge and responsible actions.

While sitting under a full-grown maple tree on the edge of a lake, I watched a yellow leaf slowly fall into the water below. It is not autumn yet. Already a leaf is falling, I wondered. The leaf dropped into the quiet lake, making a ripple as it fell. Then I thought of dear people who recently departed from our presence here on earth. Just as the leaf fell from the tree too soon, some of my family members and friends had left us a season too soon.

Although gone now, they left behind positive ripple effects, for they lived in a manner that was pleasing to God. They lived desiring to obey and please him.

I was reminded that every good gift comes from God. All of our days and years on this earth are a gift from God.

There is a saying, "God's clock keeps perfect time though it may not be our time." We may not understand why things happen when they do. There may be days of grief and hardship. We may see trouble and evil in our lifetime. Yet we can move forward and make every day count.

As we strive to use our days wisely, we need to follow God's leading. Moses is an example of someone who needed to discover God's timetable for him.

In the Bible the book of Exodus tells how the Israelite people suffered as slaves in Egypt. Pharaoh demanded the slaves make bricks for his storehouses and palaces. If the daily quota wasn't met they were whipped. When the slaves complained, they were required to do more work and even harder work.

Pharaoh ordered families to drown the male children at birth. It was during these killings that Moses was born. The midwives disobeyed Pharaoh's order, saving this baby.

Moses, the son of Israelite slaves, was adopted and reared in the Egyptian palace. He was well versed in the history and the culture of his era. He was also well aware that his fellow Israelites had spent four hundred years in bondage in Egypt. Burdened by the mistreatment and affliction of his people, Moses had an innate desire to liberate them.

One day when Moses was visiting his fellow Israelites at a work site, he saw an Egyptian slave master beating an Israelite slave. He believed the mistreatment and hard labor of his own people was unfair. Showing his impetuousness, he killed the Egyptian slave master. As a result of his brazen and hasty action, Moses was forced to leave the comforts of his home and flee to the wilderness. Humbled, he had to face the consequences of his deed.

Moses lived a quiet life in the desert for forty years. He tended the flock of Jethro his father-in-law, the priest of Midian. It was during this time that God worked in Moses's life, developing him for a very important calling. During those years, wisdom and discernment were honed. Moses was being prepared for forty years of epic service. Sometimes it's necessary to wait for God's timing to proceed.

Eventually an angel appeared to Moses saying, "I have indeed seen the oppression of my people in Egypt. I have heard their groaning and have come down to set them free. Now come, I will send you back to Egypt."[1] At that time, God chose Moses, a person who had doubts about his ability to lead. But God told him, "I will be with you. . . . It is I who have sent you."[2]

As a younger and brash young man, Moses had not waited for God's leading to help his people. But after a long season Moses was willing to be a servant of God. He learned God likes time to work. He also discovered God's timing is not always our timing. Finally, Moses was ready to lead the people of Israel out of Egypt. God would miraculously intervene to free them.

Moses was continually learning to trust and love God. Psalm 90 is one of several prayers of Moses. He said, "Satisfy us in the morning with your unfailing love, that we may sing for joy and be glad all our days."[3] Throughout our lives we can experience God's unfailing love. His goodness and mercy are with us all our days. Moses concluded the psalm with these words, "May the favor of the Lord our God rest upon us; establish the work of our hands for us—yes, establish the work of our hands."[4]

We may have a sense of uncertainty about our future. We do not really know what tomorrow will bring. However, we do know there is a relationship between the choices we make and the results of our choices.

The apostle James stated that we should not boast about tomorrow. "You do not even know what will happen tomorrow. What is your life? You are a mist that appears for a little while and then vanishes."[5] James discouraged believers from living a presumptuous and boastful life. Instead, he encouraged purposeful living, where believers seek to honor and please God.

Could this be a season in your life when you can bloom in an area of fruitfulness? Can you make a difference where you are?

Let's consider how we can redeem the time. As our days quickly pass by, we can make the most of our opportunities. Recognizing that our lives are finite, we can strive to make every day count and live each day to the fullest. And may God's gracious favor rest upon us.

Prayer

Father in heaven, blessed be your name throughout all
generations. As I live each day, help me be a good steward
of my time. Help me be more diligent in how I live
out my days and years. I set my affections on you, dwelling
in your words of wisdom. Amen.

Scripture for Further Meditation

Ecclesiastes 1:4–5; 2 Corinthians 6:1–2; Ephesians 5:15–17;
1 Timothy 4:8

Takeaway

When you live for God, spend your days as you should.
Your time on earth is a gift from him.

CHAPTER 25

Turn Fear into Faith

"For God did not give us a spirit of timidity, but a spirit of power,
of love and of self-discipline."

2 TIMOTHY 1:7

Can you recall times when fear caused you to worry and feel powerless?

Fear is a universal feeling that touches all of our lives. It is the feeling we have when danger, pain, or trouble is near. It is the emotion of being worried, uneasy, or anxious.

All of us have to learn to deal with fear in our life. It is an inherent weakness that comes to us and puts blinders on us, often putting doubts and obstacles in our path. If we give in to fear, it will affect our thoughts and actions. It will rob us of a better way to live. It can hold us back from living a victorious life.

Even as adults, fear can overtake and overwhelm us, whether real or not. There could be a fear of change, such as moving or losing a job. Perhaps there is a fear of failure, loneliness, or death.

Instead, we must feed our faith, believing what God says and Jesus says in the Scriptures. We can accept the integrity of the Word of God.

I recall the Old Testament story of King Jehoshaphat. Second Chronicles 20 tells the fascinating story of how he stood strong and overcame his fears.

Jehoshaphat, the king of Judah, set his heart to seek and please God. Living in Jerusalem, he reached out to the people who resided in the areas as far north as the hill country. These people had set aside their old ways and had turned back to the God of their fathers. So King Jehoshaphat appointed judges for the people, setting up a system of laws and justice.

At this time the king heard that there was a vast army from Moab and Ammon coming to make war against him and the people of Judah. Alarmed, he called the citizens from Judah—men, women, and children—to come together to fast and seek the Lord God for help. Coming from every town in Judah and from Jerusalem, the citizens assembled in the courtyard of the temple. Helpless and fearful, the king cried out to God for help. In his prayer, the king began with adoration of God and remembrance of what he had done for them. The king presented their problem and thanked God for helping them. He prayed, "We have no power to face this vast army that is attacking us. We do not know what to do, but our eyes are upon you."[1]

Then God told the king and the people of Judah: "Do not be afraid or discouraged because of this vast army. For the battle is not yours, but God's."[2] King Jehoshaphat then told the men they would not have to fight the battle. But they were to be prepared and stand firm against the army. They were to move forward and move on in faith.

Although the people were afraid, they were encouraged by this promise. Early the next morning the army of Judah left for the wilderness of Tekoa. As they were leaving, the king told the people to have faith in their God. Then he assigned men to lead the march by singing and praising God.

At last the men of Judah reached the place that overlooked the desert. They could see the vast army in the distance. But amazingly, there was no need to fight them. God had delivered on his promise. For while the men of Judah had been singing praises, the Lord had caused the enemy armies who were invading Judah to fight among themselves. Their enemies had destroyed each other. The people of Judah had been kept from harm and loss.

The people of Judah had not neglected to thank God. A day earlier, when the assembly of Judah and Jerusalem met at the temple, they had presented their problem to God and asked him for help. Even before the answer came, they prayed with thankfulness.

They also thanked God after he delivered them from the vast army coming against them. The people of Judah returned joyfully to Jerusalem and went to the temple to thank God. Victorious, they prayed again with thankfulness in their hearts.

When you are facing a problem or fear, where is your focus? Is it on yourself or God?

Fear often causes us to feel overwhelmed and to be ineffective. We don't like to dwell on those times, do we? Fear can accentuate the obstacles in life. Insecurity, fear, and doubt hold us back. But at these times we need to look to God for his help and strength. Try handing over the fears to God. Along with prayers for help, it is important to thank God for what he is going to do.

What are some concerns that cause you to have fear today? Remember that God helps us in our weakness.[3] We have his mighty power to deal with problems. He gives us the courage and insight to go on. If we belong to him and put our life and family in his care, we know we will be secure in his care.

The apostle Paul said, "God did not give us a spirit of timidity, but a spirit of power, of love and of self-discipline.[4] This verse says God wants us to find the answers to our specific situation, even while we fear. Our loving Father is faithful to give us what we need to replace fear with courage and sound judgment.

We have faith, not in positive thinking nor in ourselves, but in God. It comes from a desire to have a close relationship with him. At times we may fail to acknowledge that our all-powerful God is helping to fight our battles, whether big or small. But ultimately faith that moves forward triumphs.

Prayer

Dear God, when I am fearful, calm my fears, letting me know you are in control. Lead me in the way I should go, giving me sound judgment and strength. Amen.

Scripture for Further Meditation

Psalm 118:15–17; Luke 18:27; 2 Corinthians 12:9

Takeaway

When you live for God you can have confidence in him to help you face your fears.

CHAPTER 26

Serve God

"For we are God's fellow workers."

1 CORINTHIANS 3:9

H. G. Bosch wrote, "Christians are saved to serve!" Most Christians would agree with that statement. Would you say you are a person who serves God and others, or an idle person?

During the times of the prophet Malachi, the people of Jerusalem were content to live in their idle ways. Malachi noticed the people were merely going through the motions when it came to their faith. They still had the rituals of their religion. However, they had become lukewarm toward God. Malachi tried to awaken the people from their aimless living.

Malachi said the people of Israel had turned away from keeping God's ordinances. The people wondered if God even loved them. And it showed in their actions since they did not honor him as the Lord Almighty. But God reminded them of his love for them in the past. He still remembered them and loved them.

Wondering what they had gained from following God, they had a list of complaints. The people thought it was useless to serve God. They had doubts about certain aspects of their religion and it overshadowed their hearts. Their problems and attitudes showed through. It was evident that the people no longer feared God nor wanted to serve him. Israel's hope in God had faded.

Then God told them, "Return to me, and I will return to you."[1] God reminded the people that he did notice how they lived. He said he did see the difference "between the righteous and the wicked, between those who serve God and those who do not."[2]

We know when we move toward God he will move toward us. When we turn wholeheartedly to him we can expect to receive his blessings. How we live now matters, and it will also matter later. God will remember our works.

Jesus took on the nature of a servant. He washed his disciples' feet. He met privately at night with Nicodemus, a religious leader who had questions for the rabbi. He took time to visit with a Samaritan woman at the well.

Jesus came to serve others, not to be served. Many accounts tell of him spending time in prayer with his heavenly Father. While he served on earth, he gained spiritual strength and sought daily guidance from his Father.

Who can serve God? People who know him and love him. When we focus on living for God we are motivated to serve him. When we come to him with a sincere heart we are available for him to use us. Jesus said, "Whoever serves me must follow me; and where I am, my servant also will be. My Father will honor the one who serves me."[3]

When we serve God as maturing believers, we must be able to know right from wrong and good from evil. Some Christians have not been learning basic truths of the Word. It is essential to receive a solid foundation in the truths of God.

The apostle Paul reminded Timothy to be a worker of whom God would approve. He said, "Do your best to present yourself to God as one approved, a workman who does not need to be ashamed and who correctly handles the word of truth."[4]

The Greek word for minister is *servant*. Servants are ambassadors of Christ. Paul said, "As we have opportunity, let us do good to all people, especially to those who belong to the family of believers."[5] We serve one another and we serve those who are not believers. This was exemplified in the first church.

How are your abilities being used to serve others, believers and unbelievers?

God works in us as we yield our lives to him. We are servants of righteousness, and he wants us to act according to his ways. That is why spending time in the Word is important. Paul said, "The word of God . . . is at work in you who believe."[6] Continue to strive to understand the Bible. It nourishes us. As we dwell in it, the Holy Spirit helps us understand God's ways and truths.

As God works in us, he also works through us. Since he cares for us, he equips us "with everything good for doing his will."[7] He empowers us as we serve him. "We are God's workmanship, created in Christ Jesus to do good works."[8]

After we become Christians, God expects us to work for him. His goodness is reflected as we do good to others. As we have opportunity, let us show the fruit of goodness to others.

Before Jesus departed to heaven, he told the believers they would receive power. He has given us his excellent power to work within us, helping us. His indwelling Holy Spirit is the source of victory. Besides empowering for improved Christian living, the Holy Spirit empowers for greater service.

There are different kinds of gifts and service. They all come from the same Lord. "Each one should use whatever gift he has received to serve others, faithfully administering God's grace in its various forms."[9] God works through us as we use our gifts.

In 2 Corinthians Paul reminded the believers to rely on God's authority as they lived for him. Believers serve with power, having the amazing treasure of the gospel message to share. We are reminded that it is the wind that turns the windmill, and not the other way around. In the same way, it is the Holy Spirit that is powerful to do the work of God, not the person. Paul also told believers to minister with praise and thanksgiving. It is evident that worship and giving thanks lead to stronger faith and obedience. Lastly, they are to serve with persistence, not giving up, for they are being renewed every day.[10]

To grow and become spiritually healthy we must be aware of our spiritual gifts and use them. They are to be used in love and in service. Our gifts and abilities come to us by God's grace, to be used for his glory.

Are you useful in serving others? If you're not serving yet, you can begin by doing the small things now.

We have different roles as leaders, workers, parents, or children. Whatever role we have, we can share in the well-being of others. As we help others, we grow spiritually and build each other up in love. Ultimately, we also please and serve God.

Prayer
Dear Lord, thank you that I belong to you. I want my life
to show my devotion to you. Give me wisdom to know
how I can serve you and others better. Amen.

Scripture for Further Meditation
Luke 11:28; 2 Corinthians 5:20; Ephesians 3:20–23; Philippians 2:13

Takeaway
When you live for God, you show your availability to serve him.

CHAPTER 27

Stand Prepared and Ready

"Stand firm then, with the belt of truth buckled around your waist,
with the breastplate of righteousness in place,
and with your feet fitted with the readiness that comes from the gospel of peace.
In addition to all this, take up the shield of faith,
with which you can extinguish all the flaming arrows of the evil one.
Take the helmet of salvation and the sword of the Spirit,
which is the word of God."

EPHESIANS 6:14–17

When the apostle Paul wrote to the Christians in Ephesus, he knew of their faithfulness and their love for other believers. The Ephesians had accepted the good news and were learning more of God's plan for them. Paul talked about the nature of God's universe. He wanted his readers to know they were members of God's family, adopted into a new life. Since they had access to their Father, they could be victorious.

Paul spoke about putting on the armor of God. He used the analogy of a Roman soldier. It was a familiar sight in his day to see the soldiers wearing their full armor for protection.

Paul saw the Christian life as a kind of battle. He said, we must "be strong in the Lord and in his mighty power."[1] God has provided wonderful protection to defend us in the form of a suit of armor. There is a constant spiritual battle that takes place between God and the Evil One. We are to stand prepared and be ready for spiritual combat.

In Ephesians 6, the pieces of a Roman soldier's armor help us understand how we can be protected. We are soldiers in God's army and we fight "against the spiritual forces of evil in the heavenly realms."[2] We can win the battle against the dangerous opponent by putting on the armor. If we use all of God's armor, when evil comes, having done all, we'll stand.[3] We will not be defeated, but will still be standing strong.

Paul compared each piece of the Roman soldier's armor with God's spiritual armor. Let's find out more about the suit of armor that protect us.

The Belt of Truth

The soldier's wide belt was strong. Besides protecting his vital organs, it held together the other armor pieces. With the belt fastened securely, the other pieces would remain in place. The belt was the foundation for the other protective parts.

Similarly, as we put on the belt of truth, we have a sure foundation for our Christian faith. We have the assuredness and confidence of scriptural truths. These foundational truths keep us strong and ready to face adversity. They also keep us from giving in to the beliefs of this world.

When we read and study the Bible we'll increase our knowledge. We will continue to gain knowledge by attending church, learning from pastors and teachers. We can read good books with biblical truths. But knowing and believing the truth is not enough. We must also act on it and live it every day. James said, "Do not merely listen to the word, and so deceive yourselves. Do what it says."[4]

We also wear the belt of truth by being truthful and honest in what we say and do. When we use the belt of truth, we can have a clear conscience.

The Breastplate of Righteousness

A breastplate covered the soldier's body from his neck to the waist. Covering the front and back, it was made of metal plates or chains.

Just as the breastplate protects the heart, righteousness protects the heart of the Christian. From the time we are saved God sees us having the righteousness of Jesus Christ. He is "our righteousness, holiness and redemption."[5] Allowing Christ to reign in our lives, we live as rightly and blamelessly as we can. This means being honest and good. How we choose to live is an important part of surviving in the battle for our faith.

Shoes with the Readiness of the Gospel of Peace

The soldiers wore protective shoes. They had hobnails in the soles, giving them sure footing as they walked and stood to face the enemy. Being surefooted, they did not slip.

We must have shoes that speed us on with the good news of peace. Jesus is our peace and he brings peace to the Jews and Gentiles alike. His gift of salvation fosters harmony among people.

The Shield of Faith

The Roman soldier had a large wooden shield. It was about two and a half feet across and four feet long. It gave double protection for many parts of the body. For the arrows of the enemy to get to the soldier, they needed to get past the shield first. The side of the shield was made to connect together with the shields of other soldiers. This made a wall of protection as soldiers stood shoulder to shoulder, their shields side-by-side.

For added protection soldiers covered the wooden shields with tough leather and cloth. Soaking the shields in water, the flaming arrow from the enemy would hit the wet shield and go out. The soldiers were prepared against the flaming arrows that came toward them.

We must always have our shield of faith ready, since we do not know when the enemy will shoot fiery darts at us. Some of these darts could be doubt or other wrong thoughts. The enemy wants us to doubt God, just as Adam and Eve doubted what God told them in the garden. The Evil One wants us to doubt and question God's promises, his faithfulness, and his power. Some believers may even question their salvation. Instead, we will carry our shield of faith confidently, believing in the truths we know about God. Faith in God protects us when there is a temptation to doubt.

When we are faced with hard challenges, we are strengthened even more by standing with other believers. We connect with them through our shared faith. Together, we are even more effective at standing firm side by side.

The Helmet of Salvation

A soldier's helmet protected his head, helping to keep him safe. As Christians we wear the helmet of salvation, given to us by Jesus Christ. We must protect our mind, being careful what we put into it.

A churchgoer told his friend about the day he realized he needed to wear his helmet of salvation. He was singing hymns one Sunday morning while at the same time scenes of a movie were going though his mind. He had seen the disturbing movie the night before. It was clear to him that the movie scenes did not go along with the words he was singing. He was disappointed in himself for not worshiping God wholeheartedly that Sunday morning. And he knew God was disappointed in him.

As we are grounded in the truth, we will not be led astray. Throughout the whole week we must guard our thoughts, being careful about what enters our mind.

The Sword of the Spirit

The Roman soldier wore a short sword that was attached to his belt. It was the offensive weapon used for fighting.

The sword of the Holy Spirit is the spoken Word of God. God says we need to speak his Word. He empowers his Word. The writer of Hebrews described the spiritual sword. He said, "The word of God is living and active. Sharper than any double-edged sword, it penetrates even to dividing soul and spirit, joints and marrow; it judges the thoughts and attitudes of the heart."[6]

Jesus Christ used the sword of the Spirit when he was tempted in the wilderness and defeated the enemy. James stated, "Submit yourselves, then, to God. Resist the devil, and he will flee from you."[7] To win over sin it is important to speak God's Word. And when we speak his Word out loud, there is strength and power in it.

Prayer and Watchfulness

A good soldier is in contact with his commander. When he loses communication with him, the soldier is left on his own. The soldier is not able to rely on the commander's direction and support.

In the same way it is the continual prayers and requests to our heavenly Father that empower us to win the battles. Our communication lines need to be always open so we can have access to him about anything.

Since every Christian is on the front lines of the battle, we must be watchful and pray, being steadfast. For defense and offense we use our swords or God's spoken Word. When we stay in touch with our commander through prayer, we have the power for victory. Our chief weapon is prayer. We must be persistent in praying and keep our prayers sharp.

Have you neglected any piece of spiritual armor, setting it aside? What must you do to be ready in the battle for your faith?

If we have neglected to put on some pieces of the armor of God, it is not too late to use them. Live victoriously with the spiritual protection God offers. God has given us all the armor pieces we need to win, but it is up to us to put them on. Being alert and on guard, we must use every piece of the armor. When the battle is over, we will still be standing.

We do not need to fight the battle alone. There are other believers who stand with us, helping us remain strong. Standing with our faith in God and in the name of Jesus Christ, we are victorious.

Prayer
Almighty God, thank you for providing the spiritual armor I need to live a victorious life. Thank you for the sword of the Spirit, the spoken Word of God. Help me to always be a watchful and prayerful Christian. Keep me standing strong. In the name of Jesus, Amen.

Scripture for Further Meditation
Isaiah 11:5; 1 Timothy 1:18–19; 1 Peter 4:7; 1 Peter 5:8–10

Takeaway
When you live for God, you have the armor he's given you to stand prepared and to defeat the enemy.

PART EIGHT
Rest in Him

CHAPTER 28

God Cares for Us

"Who of you by worrying
can add a single hour to his life?"

LUKE 12:25

An English preacher Canon Guy King told the story of a little boy and his father shopping in a store. The father was loading his son with items when an observer said to the boy, "You cannot carry any more than you have got." Without hesitation the small boy replied, "Daddy knows how much I can carry."

In the same way, our heavenly Father knows how much we can carry. He knows our load is not more than we can bear. As a loving Father, God's compassion and care for us will see us through.

When we worry about earthly things we are holding on to them. It is in our nature to hold on. It seems we are always preoccupied about our needs or concerns.

In what area of your life do you feel insecure and apprehensive? Do you have a load that is burdensome and weighing you down?

Constantly thinking about things beyond our control is not likely to extend our life's span. In fact, continual worry creates many ill effects, impairing health and relationships. Worry takes away from what could be fuller lives. Worrying about tomorrow does not help us today. It makes us less effective and robs us of today's moments and blessings.

Several years ago I received a compelling letter from my mother. It helped change my perspective on worry.

She wrote, "I enjoyed our phone conversation the other day. It's always nice to talk with you. I know you're worried about some things. These are things you have no control over. I used to worry too. But I've learned that it doesn't do any good. Now I give my worries and concerns to God. He knows all about us, and he will work things out. Give your troubles to him, all right?"

Her letter encouraged me. My mother, wise and perceptive, was right. It doesn't make matters better by fretting about them. As time has passed, I'm learning not to worry about things I cannot control.

Jesus often cautioned against the foolishness of people who worried about earthly things. In the Sermon on the Mount he reminds us that, if God feeds the ravens, surely he will feed us, since we are of more value to him than the birds. If the flowers of the field are adequately cared for, why wouldn't our heavenly Father likewise provide for our needs?

Why should we be anxious? We have a heavenly Father who looks after us with love, happy to bestow his blessings upon us.

Jesus instructs us to focus on eternal matters instead of temporal things. He admonishes us to seek his kingdom, and our needs will be met.

We can stop worrying about things beyond our control. Instead of carrying our burdens of worry alone, we can yield our concerns to God. When we give our burdens over to him, it is amazing how happy and content we can be. We do not need to carry the load alone.

We can trust in God's faithfulness to us. He is a true friend in whom we can confide. Paul assures us: "God, who has called you into fellowship with his Son Jesus Christ our Lord, is faithful."[1] He shares our concerns and sorrows.

We can reckon on him to be faithful. The term *to reckon* is an accounting term. It means to "take into account, consider, calculate." When we reckon on God's faithfulness, in turn, our faith grows strong. We can rest in this assurance.

When King David was older, he observed that throughout his lifetime he had not seen the righteous abandoned by God. Nor had he ever seen their children begging for bread, unable to have the basics of life.[2] King David saw how the Lord took care of people who love him.

God will forever sustain us. He promises: "Even to your old age and gray hairs I am he, I am he who will sustain you. I have made you and I will carry you; I will sustain you and I will rescue you."[3] God does not stop taking care of his people.

Prayer keeps us from breaking under our load of cares. God's power working in our lives can work out our worries as we rest in him. He helps us turn our worries into prayers. As we present our requests to God, our prayers release us from our deepest concerns, freeing us. Prayer with thanksgiving strengthens our faith in God.

What are some things you are thankful for, which show God's care for you?

God is sovereign. It has been aptly said, "There is no need to pace nervously the deck of the ship of life when the Great Pilot is at the wheel." Think of the times in your life when God has taken care of you. How has he shown himself to be faithful to you, responding to your needs and concerns? Perhaps you could thank him now for his care and compassion in your life.

Prayer
All-knowing Lord, forgive me for doubting your care for me. Help me turn my worries into prayers. Thank you that I can give my concerns and requests to you. In the name of Jesus, Amen.

Scripture for Further Meditation
Psalm 55:22; Psalm 127:1–2; Isaiah 41:10; Philippians 4:19; 1 Peter 5:6–7

Takeaway
When you rest in God, you have assurance he cares for you.

CHAPTER 29

God Is Our Refuge

"I will say of the LORD,
'He is my refuge and my fortress,
my God, in whom I trust.'"

PSALM 91:2

The Old Testament and the teachings of Jesus remind us that God is our refuge. But until we face a crisis in life, it seems we do not usually think of God as a refuge. When we are hit with a personal problem or trial, it is then we become aware that we must turn to him for help.

In ancient times cities were protected with high fortified walls. A city was usually built on a hill and the wall encircled it along the natural contour of the hill. The enormous walls were made mostly of brick, built several feet thick. The high fortified walls were a fortress for the people. This was a stronghold, a place of protection and security.

Isaiah says that people who trust in the Lord are surrounded by the walls of salvation. They are like citizens who live in a strong city, fortified by its walls and ramparts. They are in a place of security. God will keep them in perfect peace whose thoughts turn to him, because they trust in him.[1]

Walls are a symbol of truth and strength. God told the prophet Jeremiah that if his people repented, he would restore them so they would serve him. He would make them "a fortified wall of bronze."[2] The people fighting against them would not overcome them. God would be with his people to rescue and save them.

In Psalm 18:1–2, David sang praises to the Lord when he was delivered from his enemies. He said, "I love you, O Lord, my strength. The Lord is my rock, my fortress and my deliverer; my God is my rock, in whom I take refuge. He is my shield and the horn of my salvation, my stronghold." David prayed that God would lead and guide him in the days ahead, for God was his fortress and strength.

The psalmist understood what most people discover to be true, sooner or later. In the end, when we feel overwhelmed we turn to the great Creator for answers. The One who made us is equally mighty to help in times of need. Given that the Creator is our companion, knowledgeable of our circumstances and needs, why not look to him? He is our helper and protector.

Facing the facts as they really are, we realize that difficult and complex matters must be given over to God. He is fully adequate to deal with them. Gone are the days of trying to handle the situations on our own. These problems can wear away at enjoying life. Do not let the circumstances get you down or hold you back.

These situations may include different struggles. One struggle may be feeling tired. Fatigue can overwhelm, wearing us down emotionally and physically. A sense of being helpless can ensue. Another struggle is feeling alone. Solitude can lead to discouragement and dejection. People may feel they aren't heard or even matter anymore. There is a sense of hopelessness.

Or maybe discouragement sets in when people see how the present circumstances are not as they used to be. They think: *Things seemed to be better then. How can anything good come from what is happening now?*

When was the last time you were discouraged? How did you handle the situation?

These struggles can be harmful to our spiritual health. If necessary, seek others who can help, especially those in the fellowship of believers. We can be encouraged again.

The teachings of the Old Testament and of Jesus call us away from being discouraged to becoming encouraged. We can trust God that there are better things ahead. He is doing miracles in our lives, big and small, and he will continue to do them. All we need to do is open our eyes and see he is at work.

Our provision comes from God. He is watching over us and he offers a place of refuge, a place of rest. We can rest in these promises:

The LORD is good, a refuge in times of trouble.
He cares for those who trust in him.[3]

God is our refuge and strength,
an ever-present help in trouble.[4]

Trust in him at all times, O people;
pour out your hearts to him,
for God is our refuge.[5]

Throughout all of these verses we find that God is sovereign. He is holy, just, and powerful. There is comfort in knowing that we can always go to him, for he cares for us.

Jesus spoke of rest for the weary. He said, "Come to me, all you who are weary and burdened, and I will give you rest. Take my yoke upon you and learn from me, for I am gentle and humble in heart, and you will find rest for your souls. For my yoke is easy and my burden is light."[6]

Another way to look at it is to consider that the safest place for us to be is in the will of God. To do this we must get right with him and live right with others. We find refuge from life's storms because of our active faith in the living God.

There is a strong connection between drawing close to him and trusting in him. The writer of Hebrews said, "Let us draw near to God with a sincere heart in full assurance of faith."[7] We can fully trust him to receive us.

He knows us and he knows our individual situation. Whether there is smooth sailing or storms and difficulties, God draws us to himself. When we trust in him completely, we can tap the reservoir of God's strength and power. Circumstances in life change, but God doesn't change.

Prayer

Dear Father, I thank you for always being my refuge. The walls of salvation protect me and I am encouraged and strengthened. Quiet my heart and mind, for you are with me. Amen.

Scripture for Further Meditation

Psalm 31:1–3; Psalm 46:1; Proverbs 18:10; Matthew 11:28–30; Hebrews 13:5–6

Takeaway

When you rest in God, he will be your safe place of refuge.

CHAPTER 30

Continue in Faith with Joy

"The Lord has done great things for us,
and we are filled with joy."

PSALM 126:3

We have heard the wonderful news of the gospel message and we have accepted it by faith. We rest completely in Jesus Christ, having believed and put our full faith in him. We are made righteous in Christ and we are his beloved.

How do we walk on? Let us move on steadfastly. Continue with the same faith and confidence as the day we trusted Christ as our Savior. As in a race, we should never give up. Remove the obstacles that get in the way and the sin that holds us back. Run with perseverance looking to Jesus, who began our faith and continues to perfect it. Jesus suffered death on the cross, knowing the joy that was before him.[1] We continue to hold firmly to our faith, for we have found the secret of contentment.

Referring to the key verse, Psalm 126:3, ponder on what God done for you. Are you amazed at all he has done and continues to do?

We rest in God's grace toward us. Just as God supplied the Israelites in the Desert of Sinai with manna, he daily provides us with his grace and love. As God's children we have gained access to this never-ending grace, sharing in its riches.

Consider the many ways he has provided for our needs. We see God's goodness in what he has done for us and is still doing for us. We feel gratitude, giving him our thanks and praise.

God has poured out gladness upon us. The gladness he gives perpetually satisfies. He leads us forward in ease and contentment.

There is joy in celebrating the wonders of God. Consider the beauty and greatness of his creation. Ponder his handiwork in the amazing universe. In his creation we see grand mountains, forests, oceans, and skies. Beautiful sunrises and sunsets over the earth continue to amaze us. Observe the cycle of life in countless animals and plants. Celebrate the miracle of life.

There is joy in salvation. God brings joy by redeeming us and showing us his love through his only begotten Son. The sinner becomes a child of God and his citizenship is now in heaven. We know when a sinner trusts Christ there is a celebration in heaven, with the angels rejoicing.

Before Jesus died at Calvary, he told his followers they could be filled with his joy by living within his love. He said, "If you obey my commands, you will remain in my love, just as I have obeyed my Father's commands and remain in his love. I have told you this so that my joy may be in you and that your joy may be complete."[2]

There is joy in worshiping and serving God. Joy is a fruit of the Holy Spirit. This joy brings strength, sustaining us and keeping us steadfast.

A key to experiencing joy is in how the Christian thinks—one's attitude. How we cultivate the mind leads to how much or how little joy we have. In the book of Philippians, the apostle Paul described the mind of joyful Christians. They are single-minded, spiritually minded, and have a secure mind.

Christians who experience joy and gladness are single-minded. Paul said that no matter what the circumstances, they live for Christ, living to please him.[3] There is single-hearted devotion to him. They let go of the thought that they must struggle on their own. They enjoy strong fellowship with Christ, enjoying the fruit of right living. Their names are written in the Book of Life, since they have believed in him.

Christians who experience joy are spiritually minded. They see things pertaining to this world from God's point of view. They live with the future in mind. Living with eternity's values in view, they serve Christ. They are disciplined and avoid worldly distractions that get in the way of spiritual progress. Paul explained, "I press on toward the goal to win the prize for which God has called me heavenward in Christ Jesus."[4] Knowing their citizenship is in heaven, Christians look forward to meeting their Savior one day. Drawing upon the promises and power of God, nothing robs them of their joy.

Finally, Christians who experience joy have a secure mind. Paul told the believers in Philippi they did not need to worry. He said, "Do not be anxious about anything, but in everything, by prayer and petition with thanksgiving, present your requests to God. And the peace of God, which transcends all understanding, will guard your hearts and your minds in Christ Jesus."[5] It is reassuring to know that God's peace guards our hearts and minds. Knowing his peace stands guard, we must do our part to avoid wrong thoughts.

Then Paul described in detail the right things to think about. He said, "Whatever is true, whatever is noble, whatever is right, whatever is pure, whatever is lovely, whatever is admirable—if anything is excellent or praiseworthy—think about such things."[6] It is best and worthwhile to fix our thoughts on these things.

How can you increase joy in your Christian life?

We have a living hope through Christ's resurrection. We are kept and protected by the power of God throughout our lives. We have a mind-set of hope for the future. So we go on, knowing God gives us his power and strength in life's journey.

Prayer
Lord of grace, you are a great God, One who loves me and shows your goodness to me. Thank you for the joy of salvation. Continue to lead me in the paths of righteousness. Amen.

Scripture for Further Meditation
Psalm 35:9; Matthew 28:18–20; 2 Timothy 4:8; Hebrews 4:14–16

Takeaway
When you rest in God, continuing with the same faith, he will keep you spiritually strong.

CHAPTER 31

Enter His Rest

"Come to me, all you who are weary and burdened,
and I will give you rest."

MATTHEW 11:28

Just as the sea does not rest because it is the sea, we also find it natural to hold onto our cares and concerns. At times we hold onto unbelief in what God can do. We may tell others we're trusting God. But deep down we may be feeling burdened about something. It continues to gnaw at us and steal our peace.

When I was a teen I sat with my friends during the worship service at church. One Sunday at the end of the sermon, my friend Tanya gently nudged me.

"Will you go with me to the front of the church?" she asked. "I'd like you to pray with me." She appeared to be troubled about something.

So we went together to the altar and we prayed together. I was glad to offer my support and thought she had received the assurance she was looking for.

A few months later as the pastor finished the sermon, Tanya asked me again to go with her to the front of the church to pray. She appeared distraught. I accompanied her to the altar of the large church and prayed with her.

That was not the last time we prayed together at the end of the morning service. Tanya was struggling in her spiritual life. She was holding on to her unbelief and doubt.

At the time she was having trouble finding rest in her soul. She was wrestling with matters that affected her walk with God. I do not recall the details of her struggle, but I know she was hoping to find peace in her life.

Have you ever been in a dark place, just trying to hold onto God? God loves us, even in the midst of our doubt and troubling times. He hasn't turned his back on us. He wants to be reconciled with us.

Jeremiah was a messenger to the people of Israel, but they were not listening to him. They had forsaken God. In fact, Jeremiah was troubled, for there was not one upright and honest person in Jerusalem.

When the people of Israel were forsaking God, the word of the Lord came to the prophet Jeremiah. He said to the people, "Hear the word of the Lord, O house of Jacob, all you clans of the house of Israel. . . . My people have committed two sins: They have forsaken me, the spring of living water, and have dug their own cisterns, broken cisterns that cannot hold water."[1]

Jerusalem became a city under siege. There was no peace there. The people were forced to face their reality. It seemed there was not much hope for them.

At that time Jeremiah boldly presented the people with a plan of action. Speaking to the people, he conveyed the words of the Lord to them. He said, "This is what the Lord says: 'Stand at the crossroads and look; ask for the ancient paths, ask where the good way is, and walk in it, and you will find rest for your souls.'"[2]

Consider this: God told the people to act. *Stand* at the crossroads of alternatives and examine the options. *Ask* for the ways that worked long ago and still work today. *Ask* for the good and right way. Then *go that way* and discover rest for your souls.

Reading the Bible has helped us find the ancient and good paths. These paths are the well-trod paths for us to follow today. When we walk the good way there is peace. Isaiah says, "The fruit of righteousness will be peace; the effect of righteousness will be quietness and confidence forever."[3]

The writer of Hebrews aptly describes the rest that is ours when we put our full faith in Jesus Christ. He says, "The message they heard was of no value to them, because those who heard did not combine it with faith. Now we who have believed enter that rest."[4] We can rest entirely in him, having confidence in him.

We cease striving. There is "a Sabbath-rest for the people of God; for anyone who enters God's rest also rests from his own work, just as God did from his."[5] We give up the thought that we must struggle on our own to become more holy. Instead, we willingly enter that rest that is already lovingly gifted to us by our Father.

When we rest we stop holding on to our burdens. It's time to lighten our load and to let go of our fears. We let go of our self-centeredness which is often the source of our grief. We can tell God about our concerns and then leave the outcome to him. He will see us through.

When we rest in him we can have victory in our lives. I like Paul's message of triumph for believers. He said, "But now [God] has reconciled you by Christ's physical body through death to present you holy in his sight, without blemish and free from accusation—if you continue in your faith, established and firm, not moved from the hope held out in the gospel."[6] We have the assurance of victory.

Before leaving his disciples, Jesus had final instructions for them. The instructions came with a promise. He said, "Go and make disciples of all nations, baptizing them in the name of the Father and of the Son and of the Holy Spirit, and teaching them to obey everything I have commanded you. And surely I am with you always, to the very end of the age."[7]

In Jesus' final days on earth he comforted his disciples, promising the Holy Spirit would teach them and comfort them. Jesus said, "Peace I leave with you; my peace I give you. I do not give to you as the world gives. Do not let your hearts be troubled and do not be afraid."[8]

This peace is given to us and it is ours forever. It springs from resting completely in God.

Prayer

Dear God, thank you for your unending love for me. Forgive me for my unbelief. I know when I am weary you will give me strength and peace. May your goodness and mercy follow me all the days of my life. Amen.

Scripture for Further Meditation

Isaiah 32:18; Isaiah 48:17–18; Jeremiah 6:16; Ephesians 6:14–15

Takeaway

When you rest in God, he will show his love to you and give you ultimate triumph.

Notes

CHAPTER 1
1. Hebrews 11:6
2. John 4:9
3. John 4:10
4. John 4:14
5. John 4:17
6. John 4:23
7. John 4:25
8. John 4:26
9. John 11:25–26
10. 2 Peter 3:9
11. Matthew 5:6

CHAPTER 2
1. Isaiah 59:2
2. Romans 3:23
3. Romans 8:3
4. John 19:30
5. John 1:17
6. Isaiah 53:6
7. 1 Timothy 2:4–6
8. George Duncan, *Every Day with Jesus* (Minneapolis, MN: World Wide Publications, 1984), 237.
9. Romans 6:11–12, 14
10. Hebrews 8:12

CHAPTER 3
1. Acts 16:30
2. Acts 16:31
3. Acts 16:34
4. Romans 1:16
5. Colossians 1:13
6. Romans 7:24–25
7. Romans 10:9
8. 2 Corinthians 5:17
9. John 15:10–11
10. John 3:3
11. F. B. Meyer, *The Christ Life for Your Life* (Chicago: Moody Press), 77.

CHAPTER 4
1. Proverbs 24:3
2. Proverbs 4:5–6
3. James 1:25
4. 2 Corinthians 5:14–15
5. Hebrews 11:1

CHAPTER 5
1. Matthew 8:25–26
2. Isaiah 9:6
3. John 14:27
4. Ephesians 6:15
5. Psalm 37:25
6. Romans 10:17
7. Psalm 4:8
8. Psalm 9:10
9. Isaiah 26:3
10. John 14:1
11. Hebrews 13:5
12. Anonymous, *Bread for Each Day* (Grand Rapids: Radio Bible Class, 1962), September 26.

CHAPTER 6
1. Psalm 37:7
2. Psalm 62:1
3. Psalm 40:5
4. Psalm 46:10
5. Psalm 32:8
6. Psalm 66:18–19
7. Isaiah 43:11–12
8. Numbers 6:24–26

CHAPTER 7
1. Genesis 2:7
2. Isaiah 45:9
3. Jeremiah 18:4
4. Romans 9:20–21, 23–24
5. Galatians 3:3
6. Galatians 4:19
7. 2 Corinthians 3:18 TLB
8. 2 Corinthians 4:7
9. 2 Timothy 2:21 NASB
10. Philippians 1:6

CHAPTER 8

1. 1 Corinthians 13:4–8
2. 1 John 3:14
3. 1 John 4:19
4. *The New Compact Bible Dictionary*
5. 1 Peter 2:1
6. John 13:35

CHAPTER 9

1. Matthew 13:19
2. 2 Timothy 3:16–17
3. John 8:31–32
4. 1 Corinthians 3:1–3
5. Colossians 2:6–7
6. Matthew 4:4
7. 1 Thessalonians 2:13
8. Acts 2:37
9. Luke 4:1–13
10. Hebrews 4:12
11. Psalm 119:10–11
12. Joshua 1:8
13. Romans 12:2

CHAPTER 10

1. 1 Corinthians 2:14
2. Jeremiah 17:9
3. Colossians 3:10
4. 1 John 3:9
5. Romans 12:2
6. Ephesians 4:22–24
7. Ephesians 4:31–32

CHAPTER 11

1. Proverbs 15:1–2
2. Proverbs 15:4
3. Proverbs 15:18
4. Proverbs15:23
5. James 3:13
6. Psalm 19:14

CHAPTER 12

1. Psalm1:1
2. Psalm1:2
3. Psalm 1:3
4. Psalm 1:4
5. Jeremiah 17:7
6. Jeremiah 17:5–6
7. Galatians 5:22–23
8. John 15:5
9. Ephesians 3:16–18

CHAPTER 13

1. 2 Peter 1:3–4
2. John 1:12
3. Ephesians 1:13–14
4. Romans 8:14
5. Hebrews 13:5
6. 1 John 2:20
7. 1 John 2:1
8. See 1 John 2:15; 2:29; 3:9; 4:7; 5:1; 5:5.
9. 1 John 3:2
10. 1 John 2:28
11. Philippians 3:21
12. 1 Corinthians 15:51–52
13. 1 Corinthians 15:54

CHAPTER 14

1. Romans 8:15
2. Jeremiah 33:3
3. Luke 11:9
4. John 14:13
5. Romans 10:13
6. Luke 18:7
7. Hebrews 4:16
8. 1 Thessalonians 5:16–18
9. 1 Peter 5:8
10. Matthew 6:9–13
11. John 14:10
12. See Luke 6:12–13; 22:32; John 17:20.
13. Luke 23:34
14. 2 Peter 3:9

CHAPTER 15

1. Galatians 2:21
2. 2 Corinthians 12:9
3. Isaiah 55:6–7
4. Micah 6:8
5. 1 Peter 1:3
6. Luke 23:39–43 TLB
7. Psalm 119:165
8. Matthew 5:9 KJV
9. Romans 12:18; 14:19
10. Philippians 4:7

CHAPTER 16

1. Psalm 143:4–6
2. Ray Comfort, *Spurgeon Gold* (Gainesville, FL: Bridge-Logos, 2005), 113.
3. Hosea 4:1

4. Hosea 6:3
5. 1 Peter 1:22
6. John 15:10
7. Psalm 42:2

CHAPTER 17
1. Proverbs 4:23 NASB
2. Andrew Murray, *The Best of Andrew Murray: 120 Devotions to Nurture Your Spirit and Refresh Your Soul* (Colorado Springs: David C. Cook, 2005).
3. Psalm 51:10
4. Matthew 5:8
5. Luke 6:45
6. Anonymous, *Bread for Each Day* (Grand Rapids: Radio Bible Class, 1962), December 3.

CHAPTER 18
1. John 4:23–24
2. Psalm107:8–9
3. Hebrews 13:15
4. Romans 1:20
5. 1 Thessalonians 5:17

CHAPTER 19
1. A. B. Simpson, *Days of Heaven on Earth* (Harrisburg, PA: Christian Publications, Inc., 1945), 252.
2. Ephesians 5:26
3. Psalm 51:10–12
4. See Romans 6:22.
5. Jeremiah 17:9–10
6. Titus 2:11–12
7. Philippians 1:10
8. Philippians 2:13 TLB
9. See Philippians 4:7–8.
10. Psalm 24:3–5
11. 1 John 3:21–22

CHAPTER 20
1. Isaiah 40:28–29
2. Exodus 19:4
3. Psalm 103:5
4. Psalm 33:20–22
5. See Hebrews 6:19.

CHAPTER 21
1. See Isaiah 53:6.

2. See Isaiah 40:11.
3. Matthew 9:36
4. Luke 15:7
5. John 10:11
6. John 10:9–10
7. John 10:28
8. See 1 Peter 2:25.
9. 1 Peter 5:1

CHAPTER 22
1. Luke 24:32

CHAPTER 23
1. See John 8:12.
2. Luke 1:79
3. Luke 2:30–32
4. Colossians 1:21–22
5. 1 Peter 2:9
6. 2 Corinthians 4:4
7. Acts 26:17–18
8. See Matthew 5:16.
9. Psalm 119:105
10. 1 John 1:6–7
11. Ephesians 5:8–10

CHAPTER 24
1. Acts 7:34
2. Exodus 3:12
3. Psalm 90:14
4. Psalm 90:17
5. James 4:14

CHAPTER 25
1. 2 Chronicles 20:12
2. 2 Chronicles 20:15
3. Romans 8:26
4. 2 Timothy 1:7

CHAPTER 26
1. Malachi 3:7
2. Malachi 3:18
3. John 12:26
4. 2 Timothy 2:15
5. Galatians 6:10
6. 1 Thessalonians 2:13
7. Hebrews 13:21
8. Ephesians 2:10
9. 1 Peter 4:10
10. See 2 Corinthians 4:7, 15–16.

CHAPTER 27
1. Ephesians 6:10
2. Ephesians 6:12
3. Ephesians 6:13
4. James 1:22
5. 1 Corinthians 1:30
6. Hebrews 4:12
7. James 4:7

CHAPTER 28
1. 1 Corinthians 1:9
2. See Psalm 37:25.
3. Isaiah 46:4

CHAPTER 29
1. See Isaiah 26:1–3.
2. Jeremiah 15:20
3. Nahum 1:7
4. Psalm 46:1
5. Psalm 62:8

6. Matthew 11:28–30
7. Hebrews 10:22

CHAPTER 30
1. See Hebrews 12:1–2.
2. John 15:10–11
3. See Philippians 1:21.
4. Philippians 3:14
5. Philippians 4:6–7
6. Philippians 4:8

CHAPTER 31
1. Jeremiah 2:4, 13
2. Jeremiah 6:16
3. Isaiah 32:17
4. Hebrews 4:2–3
5. Hebrews 4:9–10
6. Colossians 1:22–23
7. Matthew 28:19–20
8. John 14:27

Acknowledgments

To these, I humbly offer my sincere *thank you*.

For my publisher Timothy Beals and the Credo House Publishers team, for their assistance and commitment to excellence. I'm grateful for Credo House Publishers partnering with me to bring my message to the readers. Thank you to my editor, Elizabeth Banks, for her skillfulness and insight.

For my parents who helped shape my faith in God. My mother, Eleanor Ross, had a profound trust in God and love for others. My father, Samuel Ross, was a steadfast and faithful minister. As a pioneer missionary in Brazil, my father helped prepare the way for many men and women to hear and learn the good news.

For my friend and prayer partner, Vici Tyson, who encouraged and prayed for me while I wrote this book.

For my heavenly Father God, who continues to show me his goodness and love.